W9-CKM-111

THEIR MOTHERS' DAUGHTERS

By Dr. Edward A. Strecker:

THEIR MOTHERS' SONS

THEIR
MOTHERS'
DAUGHTERS

EDWARD A. STRECKER, M.D.
AND
VINCENT T. LATHBURY, M.D.

J. B. LIPPINCOTT COMPANY
PHILADELPHIA & NEW YORK

COPYRIGHT © 1956 BY

EDWARD A. STRECKER AND VINCENT T. LATHBURY

FIRST EDITION

PRINTED IN THE UNITED STATES OF AMERICA

LIBRARY OF CONGRESS CATALOG CARD NUMBER 56-6419

And he said:
Your children are not your children.
They are the sons and daughters of life's longing for itself.
They come through you, but not from you,
And though they are with you, yet they belong not to you.

You may give them your love, but not your thoughts,
For they have their own thoughts.
You may house their bodies, but not their souls,
For their souls dwell in the house of tomorrow which
You cannot visit, not even in your dreams.
You may strive to be like them, but seek not to make them
   like you.
For life goes not backward nor tarries with yesterday.
You are the bows from which your children as living
   arrows are sent forth.
The Archer sees the mark upon the path of the infinite,
And He bends you with His might that His arrows may go
   swift and far.
Let your bending in the Archer's hand be for gladness;
For even as He loves the arrow that flies, so
He loves also the bow that is stable.

—THE PROPHET, Kahlil Gibran *

* Reprinted from THE PROPHET by Kahlil Gibran with permission of the publisher, Alfred A. Knopf, Inc. Copyright 1923 by Kahlil Gibran; renewal copyright 1951 by Administrators C.T.A. of Kahlil Gibran Estate, and Mary G. Gibran.

Contents

Preface

A FEW years ago, one of us wrote a book, *Their Mothers'
Sons*. The book provoked a storm of controversy and a tidal
wave of correspondence. About eighty per cent of the
letters were sensible, eagerly inquiring, favorable, and even
heart-warming. About twenty per cent were bitterly
critical and even vituperative. Many of these were un-
signed. At one bridge club, the ladies called off the usual
game of the day in order to discuss the possibility of taking
legal steps to deprive the author of his license to practice
medicine.

Sober reflection and the passage of time have led to the
conclusion that *Their Mothers' Sons* was a step in the right
direction. Many more parents and others gave serious
thought to the problems of childhood. Many sought valid
and useful information and help and applied it intelligently.
We are optimistic enough to believe that many children
who otherwise would have been denied it, were granted
the fifth and greatest of Human Freedoms, the opportunity
and the right to grow up emotionally. So shall they be
able to participate in, and in some degree to solve successfully, the complex personal and social problems of adult
life.

The author of *Their Mothers' Sons* did make at least one mistake. He wrote the right book, but in the wrong place. First things should come first. *Their Mothers' Daughters* should have been given priority. Not only in shipwrecks, but also in life, women and children should come first. For without the right kind of mature mothers and daughters, there cannot be produced the right kind of mature sons. Nor for that matter, can a sound democracy be maintained. So we are bold enough to make this book—*Their Mothers' Daughters*.

From time to time, and rather more often than we wish, we attend wedding ceremonies. Sometimes they are happy occasions for us. When we know the young people are well on the way to becoming emotionally adult man and woman, then to us, as psychiatrists, the immortal strains of the wedding march are beautiful and heart-warming. We know that the newly wed pair will meet life as it is. They will take much happiness from life but, too, they will bravely accept its responsibilities, troubles and buffets. They will stand together and come through triumphantly.

Too often, however, as psychiatrists who sadly must acquire through professional experience some capacity for prophetic vision about people and life, we are not joyful, but troubled in spirit and heavy of heart. This is when the young couple do not show promise of becoming emotionally adult. We know that the joining in wedlock does not in itself make the contracting parties capable of living mature married lives, any more than the climbing of children into a locomotive makes them capable of piloting it to its destination safely. As *Their Mothers' Sons* pointed out, the close relationship of marriage imposes such high emotional and social ideals that no husband or wife may hope to realize them fully. In fact, perfection is not desirable. However, child-wives and child-husbands fall so far short of minimal requirements that it is not even a near miss. They make a caricature of real marriage. When the officiating clergyman announces solemnly, "If any man can show just cause why they may not lawfully be joined together, let him now speak, or else hereafter forever hold his peace," we have wanted to shout loudly: "Stop! We know why they should not be lawfully joined together. That young woman cannot fulfill the conditions of the married state. She is bound tightly to her mother (or father), to her family, to the place and house in which she lives, to the lovely little room which has been 'all mine ever since I was a little girl.' All this she will love and cherish—not the young man who stands beside her at the altar."

Sometimes it seems to us we can almost see the possessive mother, living or dead, stepping between the newlyweds and saying, "You cannot have my girl. She is mine. I know what she is. I made her that way. She is mine forever."

Let not the immature mothers who have fashioned selfish, immature sons, interpret this as a *cum laude* citation. The immature husband is probably as commonly encountered as the child-wife and wreaks as much havoc. But this book is addressed to the mothers and their daughters. If we can enlist them on our side, then the battle is more than half won. Immature sons, husbands, employers, employees, citizens, will become less numerous.

Often the wedding is followed by a reception, sometimes sensible and simple, sometimes foolishly elaborate, with luxurious food and freely flowing liquid spirits. We have found that our appetites are measured by the kind of marriage that has been performed. If it has been a "tree wedding" we eat and drink heartily. In our minds a tree wedding is one in which the marital sapling has been deeply planted in mature soil and there is every reason to believe that it will grow into a healthy and strong tree, which may bend before, but will not be broken by, the winds of adverse fortune. Always we hope for a tree wedding. Too often we have to realize it is a forlorn hope. It is not a sturdy tree, but a fragile "cut-flower marriage," destined soon to wither and perish. Then we are apt to feel queasy and our appetites falter. Probably it is an unconscious psychosomatic protest. We cannot "stomach" the ill-fated marriage.

For such marriages are made of flimsy, shoddy material, not durable. It is exceedingly likely that sooner or later, and rather sooner than later, it will be glossed over and a rationalizing label, such as "cruel and barbarous treatment" will be affixed to it. Then it will be indignantly unrolled on the counter of a divorce court.

And now to *Their Mothers' Daughters*.

THEIR MOTHERS' DAUGHTERS

Questionnaire

BELOW AND on the following pages there is presented a questionnaire. It is intended not only for mothers and fathers, but also for all men and women who are interested in the welfare of children. It is suggested that before reading the book, the questions be answered. Then, after the book has been read, they should be answered again and the differences in replies noted. Some of the questions are directed more to mothers than fathers; more to women than men, but all the questions should be answered by both. If the question is addressed directly to women, men should give their opinion of what a woman should say or do, and vice versa. Differences of opinion should provide for interesting and profitable discussions. It is cautioned that the questions should not be answered on the basis of what the reader thinks the expected reply should be. What is carried out in actual practice is the real test. Many of us know the correct things to do and say, but may not carry this out in our daily living. The answers which we think are correct are on the last page of the book.

There are 90 questions. If less than 50 are answered correctly, it is "poor." From 50 to 60 is "fair." From

60 to 70 is "fairly good." From 70 to 80 is "good." From 80 to 90 is "excellent."

1. Do you think that the biological function of women, particularly the bearing and rearing of children, is more important than having a career?

2. Do you think women are inferior to men?

3. Superior to men?

4. Do you think husbands should do an equal share of the kitchen work?

5. Do you think husbands should do an equal share of the housework?

6. If a mother has to work or has a career, do you think she should be feminine in her attitude with her children?

7. Do you think the very early relationship (say in the first few weeks of the life of a child) between mother and child is unimportant for the future, provided good physical care is given?

8. Do you think children should be punished if they misbehave?

9. Do you think it should be explained to children just why they are to be punished?

10. Do you think it would be a good plan to adopt a similar plan of punishment for all your children of about the same age?

11. Do you think punishment should be delayed until the father returns from work?

12. In order to reinforce the punishment, is it a good idea to be rather cool and distant to a child for some period of time after the punishment?

13. Do you think your daughters should have teaching and experience in household budgeting?

14. Do you think the home should be "dry," with no alcohol ever served and that children should be warned frequently about the dangers of alcohol?

15. If there is social drinking in the home, should the children be kept out of the way?

16. If mother or father are seriously sick, should the sickroom be sealed from the children and the illness concealed from them?

17. Should a mother-in-law be careful to see that her married daughters' or sons' interests are protected and that they are not imposed upon by their husbands or wives?

18. If you have been badly treated by your husband and are divorced, do you think your children should be told what kind of a person their father is?

19. If there is no love life at all in her marriage and a woman is having an extramarital affair, do you think it can be completely concealed from the children?

20. Do you investigate carefully before you employ a baby-sitter?

21. If your daughter feels she is being discriminated against by her teacher, would you accept her word for it and become indignant with her teacher?

22. If your son or daughter is experiencing "puppy love," is it a good plan to make fun of it and try to laugh it out of existence?

23. Or take it very seriously and keep very close watch over your son or daughter?

24. Would you approve of your little daughters' visiting their friends and staying overnight?

25. If your daughter is married and lives in a distant city, should you visit her frequently and have her come often to visit you?

26. If your married daughter comes home after a quarrel with her husband, should you sympathize with her and urge her to remain until her husband apologizes?

27. Should you select your teen-age daughter's clothes, her hairdos, etc.?

28. Should you select your daughter's playmates and companions?

29. Or indicate decided preferences?

30. In these days young girls are busy with school duties, sport and social activities. In view of this, is it wise to excuse your daughter from household chores?

31. If you are an invalid, do you think your daughters should give up most of their personal and social lives in order to be with you and look after you?

32. Do you feel it is unladylike for your daughters to argue with each other and sometimes quarrel and do you warn them against it?

33. If you have a child (or more than one) that you cannot bear to see punished or censured—and if punished, would you secretly solace the child and reward it?

34. If a child is handicapped by some illness, perhaps the residuals of polio, should you, in order to make up for the handicap, excuse it from any discipline and should you do all you can to shield the child from any contacts which might be unpleasant?

35. The time in which we live is often described as the age of the "body Beautiful." In view of this, do you think you should instruct your daughters thoroughly and expertly in their early teens, or before, in the use of cosmetics and all the other aids to feminine pulchritude?

36. Should you try to impress your children with your intellectual attainments and achievements as an example for them?

37. If two nice young men proposed marriage to your daughter, would you urge her to marry the one who happened to be quite wealthy?

38. Would you like your seventeen-year-old daughter entered in a bathing-beauty contest?

39. Would you like your seventeen-year-old daughter to appear professionally on TV to advertise some product?

40. Would you like your youngsters to be on a quiz-kid program?

41. If you are disappointed in the sex of the new baby, do you continue to show your disappointment?

42. Do you feel that sexual relations in marriage are a duty?

43. A pleasure?

44. Do you guard the virtue of your daughter by telling her frequently of the terrible consequences of illicit sexual relations?

45. If you have encountered much frustration and unhappiness in your sexual life, should you warn your daughters against the inconsiderate demands and sexual selfishness of men?

46. Do you think frequent talks with your daughter about sex are more important for her future sexual adjust-

ment than your natural attitude and behavior about
sex?

47. Would you tell your daughters everything you know
or can find out about a woman's role in sexual life?

48. If a little girl feels inside herself a rivalry toward her
mother for the affections of her father and sometimes
expresses it in behavior, do you think it is abnormal?

49. Is it abnormal for a little girl to wish she were a boy?

50. Or imagine she can turn into a boy?

51. Do you feel women have been unfairly treated because
they have menstrual periods and males do not?

52. Or because they have to bear babies and men do not?

53. Do you blame your husband, or become angry with
him, because of these differences between the sexes?

54. In a family of several boys and only one girl, should she
be encouraged to be a tomboy?

55. When she enters into the rough play and games of
boys, is it all right to twit her at her lack of strength
and dexterity?

56. Should the boys be encouraged to refuse to let her play
with them at all?

57. Should her femininity be encouraged and should she
be made to feel that it is as important to be a girl as it is
to be a boy?

58. In the event of death in a family, let us say the death
of a mother, should the earthly finality of death be explained to a child?

59. Given a loving mother, but one who is in dire financial
straits and barely able to afford necessities, is a child
better off with the mother, than in a fine institution
where there is the acme of care?

60. If adopted when very young, should a child later on be told it has been adopted?
61. Should an adopted child be told it is illegitimate?
62. Do you approve of the usual nursery plan in lying-in hospitals where mothers see their babies relatively infrequently for short periods of time?
63. Should you insist that your young daughter dress in neat, dignified fashion and strongly oppose her wish to wear some of the outlandish clothes that the girls in her crowd wear?
64. Do you usually feel you should enter into your daughter's quarrels with other girls and arbitrate them?
65. If your daughter asked permission to bring a schoolmate of a different race and color home for dinner, should you object?
66. Do you think that babies should be kept quiet and restrained from moving about a great deal, possibly bumping themselves against furniture, etc.?
67. Do you feel that in their teens girls should be cautioned against indulging in active physical sports?
68. Reflect carefully. Do you complain to your children, or before them, about how sick and tired you feel and perhaps describe your symptoms?
69. Reflect carefully. Do you sometimes scold or punish your daughters for bad behavior which is largely based on imitation of what you yourself do or say?
70. Do you have some particular health concern, perhaps the bowel function or menstrual symptoms, which you discuss rather frequently with your daughters?
71. On the basis that they can learn later on, do you feel

that little children should be given pretty much their own way?

72. After a child has had a long and painful sickness, is it a good idea, in order to make it up to the child, to let it do as it wants, provided it is not physically harmful?

73. If your husband has done something or said something which offends you, do you cry or sulk before the children?

74. Or have a tantrum of anger?

75. If your children ask you questions about sex, perhaps the meaning of a word they have seen scribbled on a fence, is it wise to change the subject?

76. Or answer in vague terms?

77. If you discovered your little boy examining his little sister's sex organs, or her examining his, would you regard it as dangerously abnormal?

78. If your children tell you fantastic tales, obviously untrue, of what has happened to them, or act it out, are you concerned that they will become pathological liars and deal with it accordingly?

Fathers——

79. Do you think sons and daughters should know about their father's work and sometimes actually see the shop or office in which he works?

80. As a father, are you deeply disappointed because you do not have a son, only daughters?

81. Do you sometimes express your disappointment to your daughters?

82. As a father, do you think you should express frequently your love for your daughters?

83. If your little daughter asks you to promise to marry her when she grows up, do you promise you will?

84. Do you argue with your wife before the children about matters concerning them?

85. Do you think daughters and their upbringing should be chiefly the concern of the mother?

86. Do you think it is possible for a father to be overly loving and affectionate as far as his daughters are concerned?

87. If in a family crisis you feel your wife is treating a daughter unfairly, should you remain silent?

88. Or may it be advisable or even necessary to take the daughter's part?

89. Do you think it is important for small children to learn to do things perfectly?

90. Do you think a small child's feelings are too trifling and unimportant to be taken seriously?

Chapter 1

WHO AND WHAT ARE WOMEN?

A very intelligent woman said to one of us, "Who and what do they think we women are?" Noting the emphasis in her voice, I moved cautiously. It appeared that she had read various current opinions concerning her sex and had thought them over carefully.

"Well," we said, "what do you think?"

"I don't know," was her reply, "I'm certainly confused."

We, too, have read these learned opinions. We, too, are confused. Our sympathy goes out to women. We can readily understand why they should react with psychological vertigo.

Woman has been pulled this way and that by psychiatrists, psychologists, sociologists, historians, anthropologists, even by entomologists. She has been taken apart and put together again. This with complete disregard of the obvious fact that the whole is greater than the sum of its parts. Unless the entire personality of the woman is viewed, then the essence that makes her a woman is missed. By some writers woman has been placed on a pedestal so high that mere myopic man can scarcely distinguish her fluttering garments from the wings of angels. Real and mature women do not want to be angels. They want to live on an earthly plane along with men. Other writers rate women very low indeed, much inferior to men. The biological functions of women have been glorified out of all reason. Sometimes, especially when politics are involved, it would appear that a mere collection of children's birth certificates is sufficient to call forth the highest citation, without regard to the kind of product that has been issued. On the other hand, the biological functions of women have been called a shameful badge of her servitude. We are shocked at the number of young married women who ask us for information as to how to avoid *ever* becoming pregnant. And, we are more shocked at the number of mothers who encourage them.

Perhaps the most unkindest cut of all has been dealt to women by two investigators who reported to an international association that they had discovered a third sex by finding a "lack of sex difference in the hormones of the aged." The specialists said, "Many women reach this neuter gender by fifty, while men are essentially still male at sixty."

This "third sex" is growing by leaps and bounds, according to these investigators, because human beings live longer than formerly. Some day, it is said, the neuters may outnumber the two familiar sexes!

Will it never be learned that men and women cannot be reduced to a test-tube level? There are immense differences, including chemical ones and profound psychological differences which persist to the end of life. We would hesitate to fashion therapy on the neuter theory. We would not want to tell the women of fifty or more, who come to us with emotional problems strongly involving sex, that they can stop worrying since, after all, they are sexless.

Sex is so dominant that it shows its hand even amidst the devastation of deteriorating mental disease. One of us has a patient approaching her ninetieth year. She is profoundly demented, not even recognizing her own son or where she is. Yet in some obscure feminine fashion, she is able to convey that she likes to be dolled up. A little hairdo and a few ribbons and bows. When visited by the doctor, she is apt to give him a sly little wink, totally feminine.

Often one hears the fear expressed that in this country we are in danger of a matriarchy. Whether or not we "view with alarm" depends on what is meant by matriarchy. If it means the subjugation of males by females and the establishment of a sex dictatorship, then of course we are against it. If, on the other hand, it implies an extension and expansion of maternal love in its wider symbolic significance, beyond the immediate family circle, so that, for instance, there might conceivably be a determined effort to better the lot of children or to abolish war, then we are for it.

Sometimes the fear of a matriarchy and the railing against it may be the expression of a desire for it. A man of forty came to us and told a long, rather rambling story. Stripped of its veneer of rationalizing, face-saving devices, it boiled down to about this: he was unhappy, miserable. No, his wife didn't nag or complain much. She wasn't bossy. She was reasonably well satisfied with their income and station in life. No, not extravagant. Well, what then? Well, she asks him about so many things. What, for instance? Oh, well, about the children, about their schools, whether they can afford a washing machine, lots of things. Then, after vague fumbling about, "I'm not used to it. At home Mom told us what to do and we did it. No one told Mom, not even Pop. Except Granny. Mom listened to her. It worked out all right." And so on.

Combining the span of our total experience, we have known women for more than one hundred years. Sometimes—not too often—we have felt ashamed of them. More often we have felt admiration and humility. Psychiatrically, we have known women for considerably more than fifty years. We find we can still learn and still be surprised, occasionally startled.

We have formed an opinion, though it is of course not finally crystallized. No doubt in some quarters our opinion will be considered very old-fashioned, a leftover from the past. We might point out that some old things have survival value. The sexual and other functions of women are very ancient. We venture to predict that in principle our opinions, derived from experience and many other varied sources, will outlast the "isms" that are displayed in the marts of so-called modern thought.

Biologically woman is the complement of man. This is so basic that it should dissipate at least some of the purposeless comparisons between man and woman. Men and women cannot be validly compared. They should not be thought of as competitors and rivals. The accenting of rivalry introduces much unnecessary frustration and unhappiness into the relationship between the sexes. It is not worth while spending too much time on whether a boat or an automobile is the better means of transportation. So with men and women. Their use, value, functions, are in different areas and comparisons and so-called proofs of superiority lead us astray. The main function of women is to give birth to children and "make" a home in which they may be reared. The function of men is to provide the means and furnish the protection and the sharing of responsibility which makes it possible for woman to carry out her function. To bring up girl children to feel that they are not fulfilling their destiny unless they can compete successfully with men on their own terrain, makes a travesty of all that is useful, best and noblest in women. Yet, all over the country, thousands of daughters are being reared in ignorance of woman's true function and how to perform it. Many are taught to be contemptuous of it. History shows that the sturdiest and most successful races and nations have been those who for the most part were mothered by real women, able to accept and enjoy their real function. Of course, there are many instances in which some misfortune makes it necessary for a woman to leave her domain and take up a man's work. She has to become both mother and father, a most difficult assignment. Such women deserve the highest tribute, for the situation is not of their making, even though the solution is something of a makeshift, no matter how successfully it is carried out.

The dual parental performance calls for the highest degree of psychological diplomacy. Youngsters of both sexes feel uneasy about their mothers' being cast in the father role. We know one wise woman who, since the death of her husband, has been quite successful in the literary field, who makes a point of being very feminine and occasionally even a bit "helpless" when with her children. Among other things, she adorns herself with the furbelows of her sex.

It is true that the strength of a nation derives from its mothers. Yet today so many people busy themselves in trying to prove that the strength of mothers is being impugned, unless it is demonstrated that they are as "good" as men. A real man is not usually the result of being brought up by an aggressive, masculine woman; much more likely is it that he will come from the union of a masculine father and a genuinely womanly woman. A marriage in which both partners are able, willing and eager to play their true roles is indeed fruitful, psychologically and socially.

We are not trying to fence in a compound for women in which their activities are restricted to children, kitchen and church and from which they must not stray. There are many open roads to other territories. Many women's lives are determined by mandatory circumstances, death of the husband, his serious illness, failure to marry or have children, ill-fated marriage, many other things. And then there are the innumerable interests and activities of women extending into the community, the arts and professions, even into the political arena.

We think of a woman we know, intelligent and attractive, now forty-six years old. She has two lovely daughters, eighteen and twenty years old. Her husband was killed in an automobile accident ten years ago. Mrs. B. had several opportunities to remarry and almost did but finally she decided against it. She took over the management of her husband's small factory, studied the business, and has made a splendid success of it. The business is now three times as prosperous as it was at the time of her husband's death. Mrs. B.'s two daughters were graduated from high school with honors and then took business courses. They both work in the office of the factory, doing good jobs, but within the year they will be married at a double wedding to two very fine young men. In the factory Mrs. B. is all business, pleasant enough but briskly efficient. At home she is strictly feminine, loves to cook and sew and chat with her two daughters. She hopes that one or both of the sons-in-law-to-be will become interested in the factory and gradually take over its management—"Then I can go back to being a housewife. In fact I never stopped being one. It is my vocation. The factory is my avocation."

One of the authors of this book is an inveterate taxicab rider and has come to know many of the drivers. Finding out he was a doctor, one woman driver, (let us call her Mrs. M.) has told him snatches of her history from time to time. Incidentally she is a skillful and safe driver. She is about thirty-two years old and her husband, ten years older, had a stroke three years ago which left him partially paralyzed. She has a little daughter four years old. When she talks about her daughter her eyes light up and she is really pretty.

On a typical day, she gets up early, prepares breakfast for her husband and little Lucille, fixes luncheon for her husband, does other chores, drops Lucille at a good nursery school. Then she works eight hours. Then on the way home she picks up the little girl and goes home, does the housework, prepares dinner, and the little family have a pleasant evening. She tells her husband about some of the funny experiences she has had during the day: "Joe, imagine that old guy acting as though he was going to make a pass at me. I sure told him off." Once a week Mrs. M. and her husband go to the movies. She has an exchange baby-sitter arrangement with a neighbor. Her husband has unbounded admiration for her and wishes with all his heart that he could be more helpful. He does what he can. Recently he has been trying to arrange for a home job to make children's toys. This is the story of Mrs. M. She has only had a grade-school education and doesn't know much about world politics, but she is high on the honor roll of wives and mothers.

Our readers know of the many examples of the brilliant records made by women in the professions and arts, in science, in the humanities. Some of these women were and are married and have children, some childless, some widows, some separated by divorce from unhappy marriages, some unmarried. In psychiatry there is a bright, shining example in Dorothea Dix. Singlehanded and in the face of many frustrations, she did in America what Pinel did in France. She struck the chains from the insane. She lifted them from the abyss of degradation, misery and inhumanity in many state hospitals and opened the doors of their cells, so that the light of humane understanding and treatment illuminated the darkness of their lives. She will always be remembered as one of the great humanitarians of all time.

There are many women psychiatrists and we have worked with many of them. With very few exceptions it has been a very rewarding experience. Some of them are married and have children, some are unmarried. We think of one with whom we have worked intimately. For good and sufficient reasons she did not marry until late in life and there are no children. Her husband is a chemist and they are very happy and devoted to each other. They have the same avocation, sculpturing, and there is mild rivalry between them in their hobby. But more than that, the psychiatrist likes to cook and she is a very good cook and homemaker. As a psychiatrist she is splendid and particularly effective in helping teen-age girls solve their problems, especially if their problems have been created by possessive mothers. She becomes for a time their surrogate mother—kind yet firm, sensible and wise.

One of the authors knows and greatly admires a woman in Washington, deservedly highly placed in government. She is in her seventies. Her husband is dead. She has one daughter and several grandchildren. Never is there a good cause to be served and she is found wanting. One of us labored several years to correct an injustice in the service—without success. We enlisted the aid of this woman and recently legislation correcting the injustice, which she initiated and sponsored, has been passed. Many generations of children will have a better world to live in because of the untiring efforts of this woman.

It is our thought that these activities, of which we have given several examples, are sublimations, productive insofar as they come from the overflow of maternal feelings, when the direct expression of these feelings has been blocked or interrupted. It seems to us that the usefulness of such activities is in direct ratio to whether or not the drive is powered by maternal strength. We are somewhat skeptical of the enduring value of activities motivated by inner resentment of being a woman or a desire to prove that men are inferior.

What do these fine-sounding words, "powered by maternal strength," really mean? The meaning is simple. Biologically and psychologically the chief function of women is to bear and rear children. Often—and usually for very valid reasons—this cannot be accomplished or, perhaps, only incompletely accomplished. Then the drive which did not go into the fulfillment of the primary function is diverted in other directions. And sometimes the sublimation is perhaps more important than would have been the fulfillment of the original purpose. At least we have known childless women who have been more complete "mothers" than some mothers who had children. In any event, civilization would lose much, if it had to relinquish what it has gained from childless women in the sublimation of their potential maternity.

From time to time in this book, whenever the opportunity presents itself, as it does now, we should like to counsel *what can and should be done*. Here the counsel is simple—but sometimes not so easy to accomplish. Every mother should try her level best to help her daughter become a real woman. There are no safe substitutes, short cuts, or evasions. No woman goes through life without some frustration and the accumulation of at least a few mild resentments. Sometimes the frustration is very deep and the inner feeling is strongly hostile. In any event, the mother may be led into an attitude of trying to "protect" her daughter against life. This may go to the extent of inculcating into the girl's personality feelings of wariness and even suspicion toward males, including the future husband. It is a very dangerous thing to do and will lead later to serious frustrations, impassable emotional roadblocks in life, human misery. Mothers cannot live the future lives of their daughters for them. All that mothers can do, and it is much, is to help prepare them to become complete women. In this way and only in this way as real women can they be equipped to deal with life's frustrations and find happiness.

They may not have the opportunity to marry, or they may not have children, or they may become widowed. If they are real women and not spurious facsimiles, then they will be all the better secretaries, nurses, doctors, lawyers, even riveters in manufacturing plants. Let every mother help fashion her daughters into complete women and future generations will rise and call her blessed.

Each year about 1,730,000 girl babies are born in the United States. If we could be assured that even one third of them would be given the opportunity to grow up into reasonably mature, real women, then we would be very happy. Each one in her life would add something worth while. And we would know that our democratic stature, strength, and security would be immeasurably increased. The children of these women would not be deceived by the economic, social, political, and ideological false prophets of the day.

Of course we have not answered the question, "Who and What Are Women?" We did not expect to answer it. But we do hope we have discounted some of the current fallacies. Women are not inferior to men. Nor are they superior. *They are women.*

Chapter II

READERS OF *Their Mothers' Sons* will remember the chapter, "The Mother's Dilemma." It described the two facets of true motherhood, one wanting, holding, loving, fondling, nurturing and protecting the child; the other gradually releasing it into the world so that it may lead its own life. And as we emphasized the basic importance of holding and loving, so, too, did we stress the importance of emancipating. In this book we again present the dilemma of the mother. In *Their Mothers' Sons* we particularly stressed the dilemma in regard to sons. In this book we call attention to the mother-daughter dilemma. There are notable differences, as will be pointed out again in the chapter, "A Mother-Daughter Design."

1. The daughter is of the same sex as the mother. This makes the mother feel, often rightly enough, that in her thinking she can penetrate very deeply into the daughter's innermost thoughts and being. In other words, a good mother may know a lot about her boys, but with her girls she may not only know them but *feel* that she is an intimate part of them.

36

2. Unconsciously and, perhaps even a bit consciously, she may strive to bridge the gaps in her own girlhood, the mistakes, the lost opportunities, and fulfill herself in her daughter by trying to make her into a replica of herself— as she wished she had been as a girl. Fortunately this cannot be done, and when it is partially accomplished the result is not good.

3. She may feel guilty about the lapses in her behavior as a girl and as an "atonement" discipline her daughters strictly, rigidly and even cruelly.

4. The mother's early life may have been filled with disappointments, frustrations and sadness. Naturally enough, many mothers will want to shield their daughters from outrageous fortune's slings and arrows. It is all too easy to fall into the error of overprotecting them and thus deprive them of the inalienable right to develop their own personalities.

5. Sometime in her early life the daughter will be in competition with her mother for the love and affection of the father. This is discussed in other places in this book.

In some parts of the world the birth of a female child is regarded as a calamity. In our land it is usually hailed as a blessed event. But it is more than that. It is the curtain-raiser on a play of conflicting emotions in the mother, which sometimes ends in tragedy.

One hopes the girl baby will be permitted to grow up emotionally and live more or less happily ever after. Maturity is neither inborn nor inherited. It is compounded of good environment and training, unselfish parental love, an opportunity for the growth principle to expand. Immaturity, on the other hand, is caused by the absence of a good, sound foundation for the business of living. Often, if the childhood of immature women are retraced, there is the answer. If a psychiatrist could have known these women when they were little girls and particularly if he could have known their mothers, then he could have predicted the outcome, of course with some margin of error.

When we reach into our office bag of pathology, we come up with some rather unpleasant case material. Here are two women, both divorced, both neurotically disabled, both childless. Amazingly, one persuaded a doctor to do a sterilizing operation upon her in the first year of her marriage. The other has had numerous abortions. The mothers of these two women were both divorced, each had only the one child, each feared and hated pregnancy, each had several abortions.

Less serious is the instance of a woman of thirty-two, now well on her way to adjustment. Yet the first five years of her marriage were marred by frequent jealous tantrums and violent rages against her husband. Her parents are divorced. Until that happened, when she was twelve, she lived in the murky, hostile atmosphere created by her mother's berating her father about "those other women."

Again, less serious and almost solved, is the problem of a girl of eighteen. Her socially over-conscious mother constantly impressed on her that she must always say and do the correct thing, meet the "right" people, join the "right" groups. When we first met her, she was a horrible little snob. Her conflict was made rather acute by the fact that her father, whom she adored, was a self-made man without an iota of social pretense. We were much encouraged when she reported to us recently that she had had a very pleasant chat with two strange boys on a beach. From her description they were "nice," but definitely from the "wrong side of the tracks."

To take another case: probably a psychiatrist would have predicted that Vera would become an alcoholic. Both her parents were. She was given "little drinks" when she was a girl. Yet Vera is a rock-ribbed prohibitionist. In fact, a bit too rock-ribbed. Only during the past year of her rather happy married life has she permitted cocktails to be served in the home. So the psychiatrist's prediction would have been wrong. Still, four out of five is a good batting average.

Every woman who has a child, and we are thinking particularly of girl babies, has to solve an ancient dilemma. Precisely the mother's dilemma is to find the right balance between holding and releasing her daughters; between nursing them psychologically and emotionally, and weaning them. It is not a question of time sequence, one phase coming to an end and then the other phase beginning.

The two phases are more or less concurrent. Without ever withdrawing her love, the mother from the very first helps her daughter go away from her, little by little, and with guidance, gradually to make her own small decisions, then larger ones, to think and act increasingly on her own initiative. To do this intelligently and lovingly is the dilemma of the mother.

This dilemma has been accentuated rather than eased by our tightly meshed modern civilization and its complex cultures. For the girl in her future personal and social life and for our nation, the rewards for the successful solution of the dilemma are very rich; the penalty for failure is very severe. No other nation faces as great a danger of failing to resolve the mother-child relationship as the United States. No nation has a higher stake in it than we have. The stake is democratic survival.

The future behavior of the daughter derives, and is fashioned from the opposing sensations and emotions that grow from the early contacts between mother and child. The dual role of motherhood to hold and yet to release is not as contradictory as it seems. One role merges into the other. In Sidney Howard's play, *The Silver Cord*, a character says, "Have 'em, love 'em, leave 'em be." The mother gives love and pleasure and protects the child, while at the same time she is also the agent of pain, thwartings and frustrations. The dilemmas faced by both mother and child are, in good part, mutual. There emerges a precarious balance of hold and release. Whether or not the girl learns to fulfill effectively the greater give-and-take aspects of adult life depends on how well this balance is maintained. Should the child fail to achieve the ability to give and take, her own adjustment to life, society and marriage will be severely jeopardized. Her emotions will never mature, even though she may attain Phi Beta Kappa in college.

As was said in *Their Mothers' Sons*, the mother who nurses her baby must also wean it, psychologically as well as physically. The release and freeing of the child are as significant to her future as are protection and the feeling of security. It would be useless and cruel for the mother to refuse and reject the wants of her child if this process were not preceded by, and merged with, the period of holding and protecting her daughter. The girl who has learned to take, never to give, is in for a bitter lesson in life. Her mother has endowed her with a disastrous sense of false security. How will she get on in school, with her companions, as a worker, in the marriage relationship, as a mother? In all human relationships, the world drives a close bargain. It insists upon a personal and social contribution for the satisfactions it dispenses. In the early child-mother relationship there is mirrored that daughter's future. If the relationship is not good, with not enough love, or overlong-continued emotional possessiveness and selfish domination, then there results a long, sad struggle in adult life. It may not be successful. Another broken life results. Too often the early daughter-mother relationship is tragically irreversible. It has been said that most men and women are made or broken before their tenth year. There is a measure of truth in the statement.

Certainly for some months after birth, as far as the infant can know, it is still a part of the mother. But this symbiosis or union cannot be continued overlong. Figuratively speaking, some immature mothers try to continue it indefinitely, through childhood, into the teens, even into adult life.

There is a type of immature mother who uses her daughters to gain her own selfish ends. For instance, one mother we knew—and unfortunately she and her kind are not unique—would use her seven-year-old daughter as a go-between between herself and her husband. She would tell the child that he was often unpleasant and irritable to her, sarcastic and unkind, niggardly about money, never gave her presents, expected too much from her, did not realize that she was often tired and sick, etc. This was not without deliberation since she said to the child, "Tell your father if you want." The child was frightened and worried. She began to avoid her father. He loved the child and tried to get her to explain. One day when he returned from work the little girl approached him in tears and said: "Daddy, you are mean to Mummy. You are a bad man."

This kind of immature mother tries her level best to keep her daughter attached to her, even after the daughter has grown up.

The chains with which the selfish, possessive mother binds her daughter are not visible, but they are tougher than steel cables. One of us recently had a letter from a woman of thirty-five, who had just read *Their Mothers' Sons*. She wrote that she had gained insight and understanding as to what had made her mother do the things she did. The book had enabled her to understand what a long way she had come in overcoming "her" influence. Unfortunately, this knowledge was acquired too late, and as a consequence, she feels that at least ten years of her life have been wasted.

She suggested that there are probably just as many women and girls who are victims as there are men and boys.

Things went along until she was sixteen. Then they became worse and worse. The mother became a tyrant, parasite, dictator. The family situation was such that she felt as though they were on a ship without a rudder, drifting, and sooner or later would be wrecked. The father was totally ineffectual. She even ran away from home several times, but her mother always managed to find her with the help of the police and bring her back, even though she was eighteen years or older. She did this in the hope of finding a solution to family problems by getting away and being able to view things objectively. She wanted to make the break permanent, but her conscience would not allow this, for she felt she would never be able to live with herself if anything happened to her mother which she could have prevented. Finally, she realized that if she didn't leave home, she would wind up a complete wreck. Then and only then would her conscience allow her to leave. She managed to keep an eye on her mother through other people.

Soon after, she started a two-year sojourn in sanatoriums because of a nervous breakdown.

At present she is employed as a delivery girl for a milliner in New York. She realizes that she has much to be thankful for, but feels that life lacks substance and purpose and that it doesn't amount to much.

Mothers of daughters can have many joys, but to realize them fully, the responsibilities must be accepted and the obligations satisfied.

The first essential of being a mother, loving the baby, happens more or less naturally and no explicit directions are needed. However, some women do not love and do not want their daughters. We know one young woman, divorced but fairly satisfactorily remarried. She is well endowed with money and her husband is quite willing to have her five-year-old daughter remain with them. However, she has decided that the little girl would be better off permanently with her former husband, who is somewhat alcoholic. "Why?" "Oh, well, he has a nice place in the country. The country is better for youngsters than cities." This woman's childhood was almost entirely in the hands of nurses, maids and governesses. The total absence of any maternal feeling denotes a very grave character defect. The maternal feeling is much older than the human female. Long before the existence of the human species, animals mothered and protected their young, as they do now. Sometimes psychotherapy—long, expensive and difficult—makes it possible to instill and replace something which was denied its natural, easy and beautiful growth in childhood. Nearly every little girl wants to be a mother. Observe her with her dolls.

We are not sure that we know exactly how to tell mothers to fulfill the second part of the mother-daughter contract of love—relinquishing their daughters. We can tell why the emancipation is not accomplished and what happens. Even though the reasons may be unconscious, they are extremely selfish. (We say "may be" since there is reason to believe that sometimes the reasons are at least partly conscious.) Often the mother is dissatisfied, feels that life has let her down emotionally, even though she may not admit it consciously. With the rationalizing pretext of wanting to protect her daughter from the hard knocks which life gave her, she feeds on the girl's emotions and binds her closely to herself. It never pays off. Very often the daughter, perhaps too late in life, comes to realize how she has been cheated by her mother, feels deeply hostile toward her unconsciously and may even come to hate and revile her openly. How much better it would be for the mother to take the long chance. In spite of her own frustrations, or rather because of them, she will help her daughter become an honest-to-God woman. Then there is a reasonable chance that later she will receive her deep love and devotion and the love of her grandchildren. It is well worth the chance.

All this sounds as though these mothers were acting consciously and deliberately in holding on to their daughters emotionally. Their behavior is almost always unconsciously motivated at the beginning and sometimes it remains unconscious throughout. However, sometimes more or less conscious motives of "secondary gain" creep in: "I will be lonely," "I would be unhappy," "I would have to take second place," "I will lose my daughter's support," etc. Perhaps they do not make the bold statement, but indicate it in some shape or fashion. It is difficult to believe, when so much has been written about the dangers of maternal possessiveness of daughters, when it is so often portrayed in the movies, on the TV screen and over the radio, when indeed it is so familiar a conversational topic, that so many women seem oblivious of what is common knowledge. Whether or not they can accept it and act on it, is difficult to answer. At least there is the opportunity to learn.

To most of us the word "relinquishment" sounds harsh and unpleasant. It sounds like giving up something we wish to retain. True, it does mean giving up, but that is not quite all there is to it. In the giving up there is often compensation. Perhaps "sublimation" is a better word. In effect, sublimation is the utilization and diverting of energies and activities no longer needed for one objective into other useful and constructive channels for objects by which they are very much needed. So it is with the relinquishment of daughters by their mothers. First, the mother partly relinquishes her daughter to her little playmates, to her schools and teachers, to her sports, to her small social activities. And she finds joy and satisfaction in seeing her daughter acquit herself well and she shares her daughter's happiness. Then may come her daughter's interest in the opposite sex—the boy across the street, other young men, then finally the young man her daughter will marry. Again the mother may find happiness in the thrill of witnessing and sharing the budding and flowering of her daughter's love life. More often than is thought, a real mother does gain a son in her daughter's husband. And that is compensation. Then there are grandchildren. In them she may relive her own maternity. And then there is the compensation of participating in community and even national interests. Here she may apply her knowledge and experience gained in her relationships with her daughters for the benefit and welfare of many children. All this would not be possible without relinquishment and sublimation. True it is that without relinquishment and sublimation life would be a mockery without worthwhile objectives. The man or woman who has nothing to live for is, psychologically, dead.

Chapter III

UNSEVERED UMBILICAL CORDS

WE WISH we did not have to write this chapter. It is not pleasant to call anyone immature. And it is doubly unpleasant to call some mothers immature, particularly since the immaturity may not be of their own making. It may have been foisted upon them by immature mothers and fathers, or it may have been imposed upon them by the exigencies of life. However, we must be realistic about it. Immaturity is present in many women. It does much harm to their children. It interferes seriously with their daughters' exercising the functions of marriage and motherhood, even in passable fashion. Therefore, it becomes an obligation to file a brief against immature mothers.

We wish people would stop blaming us for the word "mom." We did not coin the word. Probably it was first put into general use as a term of reproach by Philip Wylie in his interesting book, *A Generation of Vipers*. Wylie used the word in a rather bitter, vituperative sense, perhaps justified by the context in which he employed it. We have nothing against the word "mom" and we do not use it disparagingly, excepting occasionally to designate a dan-

47

gerously immature mother. Then it becomes a convenient word, but one to be used sparingly. The word "mom" used as a term of endearment to their mature, loving mothers by thousands of boys, girls, men and women, is not an objectionable word. We wish it could be qualified in some way so that it would not be displaced from the laudable place in our language that it deserves. Unfortunately, it has often come to mean the maternal parent who fails to prepare her offspring emotionally for living on an adult personal and social plane; who does not untie or at least loosen the emotional tie, "the silver cord," which binds her children to her; who derives emotional pleasure, approaching fulfillment, from keeping her children paddling about in a kind of psychological amniotic fluid, instead of allowing them to swim away from the maternal womb, with the increasingly strong and independent strokes of the mature adult. The immature mother does not want to teach her children to swim. She wants to keep them close, in the shallow waters within sight and touch. Sometimes she succeeds in doing this with her sons, and more often with her daughters.

The psychological mother-daughter umbilical cord is complex. The central core is love—mother-daughter love. It was designed to be and should be life-lasting. The central love core is surrounded by many strands including nurturing, protection, dependency, guiding. These are very important at the proper age but there comes a time when they should be loosened and then stripped off. The dangerously immature mother never removes them. Unconsciously she thickens and strengthens them until finally they strangle true love. This is not real mother love. It is "smother" love. Not always is the process totally unconscious. Some-times we have observed it come into conscious expression. One woman in discussing her teen-age daughter of whom she was very possessive said with shocking frankness: "Sure I am holding on to Jane. Why not? My husband left me for another woman. My son is a disappointment to me. He is married, lives far away and is engrossed in his wife and children. I am entitled to something out of life. You bet I am going to hold on to Janie."

Usually this kind of "mom" is not externally marked. Often she is charming and gracious, converses intelligently and participates in useful community projects. With her children she may be doting and sweet and seemingly self-sacrificing. However, the obverse is not uncommon. "Mom" may be hard, unrelenting, stern, self-contained or violently cruel. Underneath we are still primitive. Let us remember that in each of us there are deep instincts of violence and cruelty. Successive layers of civilization and culture have veneered our once-unrestrained instincts. We suppress, inhibit and repress them, but they are only held in leash. Apparently the leash is not too secure. How else explain the mass bloody orgies of war during the past forty years? As we have indicated, it is conceivable and some-times does happen that the loving, protective functions of mothering are overridden by cruel and violent behavior toward children. Usually women are less violent than men, but they can be just as cruel.

As we describe immature mothers later on, it will be seen that many are unhesitatingly self-sacrificing for their chil-dren. We only wish it profited the children more. One day they will have to try to get along in a world not populated by kind, doting, spoiling mothers. A columnist interested in our work, told us of bringing home what he thought were a rooster and a hen. The "rooster" turned out to be another hen. Not wishing to waste so much potential maternity, he bought a brood of chicks and distributed them equally between the two hens. One hen proved to be a mother, doing her maternal duty completely, but not standing for too much nonsense. Efficiently she taught the chicks to work and scrape for the food they needed. The other hen was a clucking mom. She worried and fussed constantly and was forever distributing feathery caresses. Her chicks treated her outrageously. The sensible mother's chicks were easy victors in scurrying for food and in tugs-of-war for worms. Soon they established their supremacy over mom's chicks in all societal matters of the chicken run.

Perhaps there is a moral. We have certain functions in common with animals and we have not disdained to bring some of them into our civilization without overmuch modification or adornment. Perhaps the function of preparing the offspring for the struggle of adult life, which animals usually perform so expertly, has some survival value.

We still wonder, for instance, about Max. He was a black, fat, lovable little puppy brought home from the laboratory after his mother had been sacrificed in the interests of science. Max did not take kindly to bottle feeding. Fortunately, in the home there was a mother cat nursing a litter of kittens. She welcomed Max to her nipples and he seized them greedily. The foster mother gave the puppy preference over her own kittens. But Max did not turn out well. As he grew older his temper became unpredictable and, often, seemingly without reason he would growl and bite. He became so vicious that he had to be destroyed. Not enough is known about animal psychology to draw any authentic conculsions but perhaps it is not too farfetched an inference to say that even in the animal world it is difficult to find a satisfactory mother substitute. Certainly in the world of babies it is extremely difficult. More and more we are coming to realize that the very early relationship between mother and baby is very important and significant for the future psychological growth and development of the child.

Silver cords vary in length. They can be quite short—leashes, in effect. They can bring a child "to heel" as quickly as a ranch hand can lasso a refractory calf and apply the branding iron. The case of the mother who proudly announced that her teen-age children had never spent a night away from home was mentioned in *Their Mothers' Sons*. "When bedtime comes, they want to be tucked in." This was her smug, if somewhat startling, conclusion.

As a rule, silver cords are a great deal longer. They may be stretched so thin as to be almost invisible, but they are amazingly strong. They give all the appearances of permitting the child a vast area of latitude in her life. If, however, the child ranges too far afield, it is remarkable how abruptly they can be drawn taut as bowstrings.

The mail, especially air mail, the telephone, the telegraph and cable provide readily available extensions of silver cords.

Here is a letter, somewhat abbreviated and edited to prevent identification, which a mother wrote to her young married daughter two thousand miles away.

"DEAR ELLIE: I know I write almost every day, as you mentioned in your last letter *almost a week ago*, when you said you were sorry you could not write more often, but you were so busy with the children. It is hard for me to realize that my very own daughter can be so busy that she cannot find time to write to her mother. Perhaps some day when you are older and your daughters are grown up, you will understand better and be lonely as I am. I miss you so much.

"Your father is busy at the office and often brings work home. He does suggest going out more, but I don't care much about it. I miss my children and sometimes feel they have forgotten me. As you know, your brother lives almost as far away as you do and I only hear from him now and then. I suspect his wife keeps him from writing more often. Maybe Jack [the daughter's husband] has asked you not to write to me.

"Not much use in talking things over with your father. He seems so well satisfied with the way you and your brother are getting along. I suppose I shouldn't, but I admit it does irritate me a bit to have him repeat so often that he is happy to have you so nicely settled. He is a great admirer of Jack's. Of course, I think Jack is a very good husband and looks after you and the children well. But I don't think he likes me. I thought he was a little cool at my last visit. Maybe he thinks four visits a year are too much. I don't agree. You see, Ellie, I happen to love you very dearly. It is nice seeing the children too. After all, I only stay a few weeks or so. When do you think you will visit us? I know it is hard to travel with young children, but after all, I am your mother.

"As I said, I am lonely. Sometimes it seems I raised you children just to have you leave when I need you most. Your father thinks I should get interested in the Ladies' Club and community things, but I guess I'm just a mother.

"I often think how nice it would be if we all lived together. Maybe not in the same house, but near enough so that we could see each other every day. I suppose that is impossible, but there is no harm wishing. What fun we could have. I suppose Jack has to do his work where there is the best opportunity, but there do seem to be lots of opportunities in his line here.

"I have just read this letter over and it sounds a little complaining. Well, I'm sorry, but I miss you.

"With love and hugs and kisses,

MOTHER

"P.S. Sound Jack out about another visit from me. Don't show him this letter."

A young woman living on the Pacific Coast and doing a good job with her marriage, with one child and expecting another, received this wire from her father in an Eastern city: "Mother dangerously sick. Come at once." In a few hours she was on a plane. Arriving at the home of her parents, she went to her mother's room and stopping at the open door, overheard this conversation between her mother and the family doctor. Her mother: "But, doctor, it must be serious. I am perfectly willing to have an operation." The doctor: "Now, Susan, calm yourself. It's nothing serious. You know the surgeon said there was nothing to operate for. All the examinations were negative.

Maybe an upset stomach. That's about all. You know how nervous you get about yourself." Mother, seeing her daughter: "Why, there is little Susie. Darling, I feel better already." And in a few days she was all well and having a wonderful visit with her daughter.

We do not pass judgment on this situation. We do not think the lady pretended to be sick, though we have known immature mothers who feigned illness to bring their children to their sides. Whether conscious or unconscious, still it was very selfish.

As a refreshing antidote to these two situations we would like to present a comedy from real life. Margie, twenty years old, was a three-months' bride. She was a little "skittery," but had the makings of a real woman. This in spite of the fact that Margie had not been a strong baby or girl, being quite anemic following scarlet fever, several ear infections and a mastoid operation. Her mother, loving and affectionate, but with her eye on Margie's future, did not let her illness deter her from helping her daughter grow up emotionally.

One day, suddenly and unexpectedly, Margie appeared at her mother's house in tears: "Mother," she sobbed, "it's no use. Bill and I can't get along. I left him for good. I'm home to stay."

The mother kissed her daughter, gave her a pat or two and said, "Tell me." Then Margie, in a voice choking with emotion, told of a difference of opinion between two nice young people, such as happens in about every marriage. "And, Mother, he cursed at me."

The mother looked very thoughtful, even though she did not have to give it much thought. Then after a nice, wise talk about the little problems of married life, how they seemed at the time much more serious than they actually were, how married people lived happily together in spite of occasional quarrels, how they later on laughed at how silly they had been. "That's the way it is with your father and mother." Then very firmly: "Margie, just unpack enough to stay the night. You are going back to Chicago tomorrow. And you are phoning Bill tonight and making up." A few more tears from Margie and, "I guess you don't want me here, Mother," and her mother replied: "I guess that's true. I always like to see you, but more than that, I want you to be home with Bill, where you should be now."

Margie did phone and make up. It was surprisingly easy. Bill was more than anxious to meet her half way. The next day Margie went home. And her good-bye kiss to her mother had in it not only love, but gratitude. All this happened more than five years ago and since then, five years of happy married life. And when Bill sees his mother-in-law, the kiss he gives her is anything but the traditional son-in-law kiss.

One thinks of the contrast of this mother with the one who wrote the first letter. One may ask, "From what kind of mothers come such missives of gloom and selfishness which may administer the *coup de grâce* to a marriage which a daughter is striving to make successful? What are the women like who write such letters—letters like the one quoted and worse—letters like slender silver cords, slender but strong enough to strangle courage?"

Chapter IV

OBSTACLES TO SUCCESSFUL MOTHERHOOD

WE DO not have the eloquence to describe the perfect mother. Fortunately it is not necessary; she does not exist. We could, from our experience as psychiatrists, describe more than one example of motherhood at its nadir, but these would be case histories from the field of abnormal psychology, and they do not belong in this book.

After all, we are less interested in the zenith and nadir of motherhood than we are in the "in-betweens." They are the audience we hope to reach. They are eager, receptive, anxious to learn. Those women who function at the peak of motherhood do not need our help. They know more about it than we do. The nadir mothers do not want our counsel. A friendly critic, after reading *Their Mothers' Sons*, said, "A good book. It should help many mothers. But if you think that it will have any effect on real dyed-in-the-wool moms, forget it. They will read the book and exclaim piously, 'Isn't it awful that there are women like that in the world? Thank God I am not that way.' "

Some women are not quite complete mothers, but they are "very near" mothers and, all in all, they do a very serviceable job. They may fail in a few areas, but they have brought their daughters far and the impetus is strong enough so that marriage or some other vocation in life adds the few needed details and gives the final nudge. One mother turned out a very fine daughter, except that the girl learned little or nothing about household economy from contact with her mother. To the mother a budget was a forbidding ogre. Charge accounts were tempting things and it was easy to forget at the time that what was bought had to be paid for—some time. She was not ill-tempered about her weakness, freely acknowledged her mistakes, tried hard to correct them. She corrected a few, but not many. The daughter had a little trouble with finance during the first six months of her marriage. Fortunately, her young husband was an accountant. He found it fun to help his wife and soon the economic ship was sailing smoothly. It is nice to record that this young woman's mother gladly accepted bookkeeping help from her daughter and profited by it. However, it should be mentioned that a mother cannot count too much on the daughter's marriage to fill in the vacuums she herself has left in her daughter's training.

In our "what can or should be done" department, it is worth noting that a little training in household budgeting, how to spend the available money to get the most satisfaction and pleasure from it, is getting to be a "must" in this day of high prices.

Besides insufficient training in household budgeting there are many other lapses in the business of being a good mother. Perhaps in themselves they are not too serious but they may add up to future trouble. A mother may habitually fail to keep the house in order, leaving things scattered about, unwashed dishes in the sink overnight, etc. Or she may be lax about reasonable personal neatness and cleanliness.

On the other hand a woman can be too neat, too clean about herself and her house. She belongs to the sisterhood of "You could eat off the floor of my house." Mrs. B. was that way. And by the time her daughter Jane was nine years old she was that way too, eagerly following in her mother's footsteps, enthusiastically wielding her little broom and duster, with furrowed brow and an eagle eye for the tiniest fleck of dust. When her father returned from work, she inspected him carefully for spots on his clothes and brushed them. Fortunately in college the influence of her roommates made Jane modify this characteristic. But some of it remained. She is reasonably happily married to a big, good-natured chap, but from time to time she scolds and nags him for dropping a little cigarette ash on the floor.

Some women just seem to meander along in life, showing lots of promise, not much fulfillment, until they become pregnant. Then they have the baby and literally burst into maturity. Their personalities expand like buds in the sun.

On the other hand, pregnancy and childbirth may have the reverse effect. Sometimes they seem to reveal a flaw in a woman's childhood, for instance, that she was entirely too much fussed over by her mother. This was the case with Betty L. In spite of her mother's oversolicitude and almost constant fussing she seemed to grow into a well-adjusted girl and young woman. Then she married. For the first two years of married life things went smoothly enough. Then came a little baby girl. Betty changed completely. She became a fussy, worried, overanxious mother about her baby—her feedings, her clothes, her teeth, a breath of air, everything. The little girl, now five years old, clings to her mother like a limpet, is afraid of strangers and is even "strange" with her father. He takes the path of least resistance and will not take a stand. It does not look too good for this little girl's future.

Pregnancy and childbirth are sharp cutting instruments which separate the chaff from the wheat, the mature from the immature. It is interesting to observe that an increasing number of young women are insisting on being allowed to experience some labor pains. Probably it is true that some conscious remembrance of childbirth gives a good start toward real motherhood.

Returning to the insurmountable stone walls which are obstacles in the path of motherhood, there is serious illness in the mother. She can scarcely function from a sickbed, though we have known some sick women who did a heroic job of holding things together. It is not, except under special circumstances, a good plan to seal off the sickroom from the children entirely. It becomes for them a chamber of threatening mystery. True, when they see their sick mother, they are upset, but probably rather less than the adults. They will be more frightened and damaged by not knowing at all what is happening; the hushing, the frantic dashing about, the grave faces of the family, the frequent visits of the doctor, the calls of the priest or minister. After all, sickness and death are as much a part of life as health and birth.

We think seeing the sick mother means a great deal to the child, both then and later on in life.

We remember a mother who was sick for several years of her life, usually in bed. Her little boy was saddened but always felt better after seeing her. Her hands were quite emaciated and he still remembers stealthily covering them with the end of the bed sheet. He was doing something for her. Many mothers, even though quite sick, are cheerful and optimistic with their children. "I just feel a little tired, darling. It will be all right." It is the offering of love.

Besides illness, there is the possibility of alcoholism—or worse, drug addiction—in the mother. Often alcoholism in the parent deals a death blow to the developing personality of a girl. The shaming of the ego before other children, in the neighborhood, later before her boy friend —such things often cannot be lived down in a lifetime. We know a fine woman in middle life who, although nearly cured of an anxiety neurosis, still occasionally suffers from severe suffocation attacks. They are traceable to an alcoholic mother. As a child this patient, left alone with her mother, often saw her in alcoholic stupor, with labored, stertorous breathing.

When one of the authors was an interne, a little girl ten years old was brought into the hospital in an alcoholic coma. She had seen her mother drinking from a whiskey bottle. When the mother was in a drunken stupor the child drank the remains of a partially filled bottle of whiskey. The child died.

The plight of the little girl whose mother is an alcoholic is pathetic. Such was the sad lot in life of Maizie C. Her father was dead. At first, when Maizie's playmates said to her, "What makes your mother talk so funny? She doesn't walk straight, does she?" the child dashed home and wept bitter tears. Later, as she grew older, she vigorously defended her mother. "Don't you say mean things about my mother. She's better than your mean old mother." Still later there were elaborately contrived explanations, "Mom has a lot of trouble with her stomach. She gets headaches and gets dizzy," etc. Fortunately the mother finally joined an Alcoholics Anonymous chapter and overcame her alcoholism. Maizie, now seventeen years old, is very happy about it but one cannot yet be sure that no permanent damage has been done to her personality.

Without wishing to be regarded as finally authoritative, we may say that we are not in favor of either a very "wet" or a very "dry" home. In some homes the alcohol flows almost as freely as the tap water. The children can hardly avoid stepping into the puddles. They observe, indeed they often note with gleeful interest, the evidences of inebriety and develop a laissez-faire attitude which is not good. A home may be very dry, that is, no alcohol is served in it. We think of "very dry" as the home in which the evil and horrors of alcohol are constantly and luridly described to the children. It leaves too much temptation to explore later on in life. We are for the home in which alcohol is served from time to time, in an environment of friendly conversation. The children are not banished behind the iron curtain of listenings and whisperings. We think fewer alcoholics are made in these situations than in the very wet or very dry home atmospheres.

In-laws may be formidable obstacles to mothers. As we look over our case material, sometimes we feel like throwing up our hands in despair and saying to young people: "Marry orphans." There are in-laws, mothers-in-law and others, who are fine and good, helpful and reliable, non-interfering. We can dismiss them from consideration, except to bless them. But there are others. They include mothers-in-law who try to destroy a promising marriage, and sometimes succeed. And rich uncles and aunts who hint that they will remember little Joe and Nancy in their wills, *provided* their names are changed to their own; that they make them long visits, that they go to certain schools, etc. Then there are grandparents who slyly bribe and perhaps try to entice children away from their parents with all sorts of wonderful gifts. One old fellow drove up to the door of his teen-age grandson's home with a beautiful, shining convertible. "Here's a little present from your grandfather." As it happened, two weeks earlier the boy had smashed up the family car by careless driving. The mother said, "No!" to the grandfather's gift. Furthermore, she inserted the iron rod of her maternal determination into her rather weak and spineless husband her "no" stuck.

The mother-in-law joke is said to be the oldest joke in the world. Unfortunately, it is not a joke. The mother-in-law, either the battle-axe kind or more frequently and more dangerously the undercover worker, can distort a marriage so that it would be better if it had never taken place. Here, our apologies to the many superb mothers-in-law who are towers of strength, understanding and selfless love. We know they are ashamed of their immature counterparts.

Once one of us, in a streetcar, overheard one woman say to another as they passed a telephone exchange: "Yes, she works there. She thought she could get my boy away from me. They split up. He's home with me now and I will take good care another one don't get him away from me."

A woman we know made very generous gifts of money, clothes and other things to her son. Nothing to his wife. Of course there was a *quid pro quo*. He had to repay in the coin of daily telephone calls and frequent and long visits to see her. "Poor William!" His "shiftless" wife didn't look after the house and keep it attractive. (She did as well as she could with four young children and an immature husband to look after.) She didn't give the poor boy the right kind of food (the food was excellent). She was always buying clothes for herself (she bought very little for herself). She didn't have to buy that evening dress when William should have a nice camel's-hair coat (an inexpensive dress, which she needed very badly; anyhow, William got his coat from his mother).

These are only a few examples from an inexhaustible stockpile of nagging complaints.

One wife was a fine, mature young woman. She loved her husband and the children. She tried her level best to persuade her husband that they could get along on what he earned. "Let's try, we can do it." Occasionally he would agree with her, but in a few days he would announce, "Next year, young Tom is going to M——," mentioning a very exclusive and expensive school. "We can't afford it," protested the wife. As usual, the answer was, "Oh, Mother will pay for it. She wants to do it."

This wife had in her the stuff of which real mothers are made. After many years of unsuccessful striving, she separated from her husband—did not divorce him. It was all very amicable. The husband was relieved. He frankly said he didn't like family responsibility. He continued to depend on his wife, visited her and the children frequently, spent many days with them. Of course, as the children grew older, they read between the lines, but never from their mother did they hear anything but the kindest things about their father. Always the mother emphasized his good qualities.

This unhappy man always felt very hostile toward his mother, at first unconsciously, then openly. He said he hated her. But he could not break away from her. The chain she had forged during his childhood was too strong. Whenever he showed any signs of breaking it, she reinforced it with money.

Not all wives have the built-in reinforcements which enable them to thwart the wrong kind of interfering mothers-in-law. Lillian R. was a nice, good-natured, rather indolent Southern girl. At nineteen she had married a young Northerner whose mother was extremely wealthy. There was one child, a girl, Daisy. Here the mother-in-law stepped in armed with determination and much cash. Mrs. R.'s husband briefly resisted the invasion and then left his wife to carry on the battle to save Daisy from being hopelessly spoiled. Mrs. R. carried out a mild counter-offensive against her mother-in-law's wiles and for a short time was very unpopular with her. Then she capitulated. She confided to a friend, "What's the use? I can't beat the old bitch. Anyhow, it's just too much trouble." So Daisy had from "Granny" just about everything. Beautiful hand-embroidered clothes, fabulously expensive imported dolls and toys, a governess, later a personal maid, an automobile with Granny's chauffeur to drive her, anything and everything for which she expressed a wish. And her mother shared in the loot. Now her mother-in-law "just adored" Mrs. R. and gave her expensive presents and jewelry. Little Daisy spent more time in Granny's mansion than in her own home. In effect her attitude toward her mother was, "I like it better at Granny's. I think she loves me more than you and Daddy do." Daisy is now sixteen years old, pretty, insolent, arrogant, unpopular in her set excepting with those boys and girls who want to bathe in the luxury that surrounds her. If anyone crosses Daisy she runs to "Granny" and tearfully tells her. In some way or another "Granny" fixes it.

We could go on about mothers-in-law, but we have said enough. Many wives (and husbands, too) caught in the mother-in-law web, know all too well what we mean. No more words are needed.

A formidable barbed-wire entanglement blocking the path of motherhood is an immature husband. Oddly enough, it is the reasonable, mature young woman who is in the greater danger of being saddled with one. Even as a girl she is strongly maternal. There is something very intriguing and provocative in mothering the helpless young male whom she is going to marry—tying his tie, brushing his hair, removing the food droppings from his clothes, telling him to pull up his socks and keep his shoes shined. Then they marry. We wish we could stop here, but our duty to American daughters, potential mothers, compels us to complete the picture.

They marry. For a time the young woman finds the outlet for her maternity in babying her husband. Then real babies begin to arrive, tiny, helpless, lovable creatures.

Now she has found the fulfillment of her womanhood, which biology ordained countless ages ago. Her six-foot baby husband and his demands begin to pall. No longer is she thrilled by calling him half a dozen times to get him up in the morning, seeing that he gets all his clothes on, feeding him his breakfast, seeing that he gets the bus in time for work. For one thing, she is too busy looking after the children.

Then the immature husband begins a campaign, the unconscious objective of which is to make his wife his mother. All kinds of tactics may be employed. Often he exercises petty tyrannies over household purchases and accounts. In a social gathering, if the company is interested in his wife's conversation, he may attempt to gain the center of the stage by interjecting some embarrassing remark. "That reminds me, dear. Do you remember the time your mother got tight and we had to take her home in a taxi?" He may even pretend to be sick, in order to get his wife's nursing attention. One immature husband we knew hid the baby from his wife. He did it only once.

The immature husband is not above having sickly love affairs with other women, the "You poor boy. Your wife doesn't understand how sensitive you are" kind. Thus he hopes unconsciously to gain his wife's maternal attention and solicitude.

If the wife is emotionally grown up, then the husband's campaign to make her his mother is doomed to failure. She may still love her husband, but she is fed up with his behavior. It is too much. When she is very busy looking after the younger children, she cannot even depend on her husband to play games with the older ones, because if he loses, he is apt to sulk.

The final outcome is dubious. There may be a divorce. There may be a compromise marriage. Sometimes, with psychiatric help, the husband may grow up enough emotionally so that he can learn moderately well and sustain his role as a mature husband and father.

There is another situation which interferes with the functioning of women as mothers, and that is the situation of the absentee husband. In civilian life sometimes V.I.P.s, men of international business, and traveling salesmen are away more than at home. (And then there are golf widows.)

We know a traveling salesman, a fine young man, able, conscientious, advancing rapidly in his work. He is basically a family man and regrets that for the next few years he will have to be "on the road" for the firm. He is married and has two children, a girl ten years old and a boy six. His wife is attractive but unhappy and suspicious. Her mother during her childhood checked on her husband —"other women." The children are troubled and anxious, particularly the daughter, Beatrice, who loves her father very much. Mrs. Blank does not go so far as to impart openly to her children unfounded suspicions that Bill is running around with other women, but little Beatrice is not a moron and long since she has correctly sensed her mother's attitude. Frequent phone calls to her husband, sometimes suspiciously, "Bill, is there anyone in the room with you? I thought I heard a woman's voice," sighs, now and then unexplained tears. Bill tried the plan of making many unscheduled phone calls to his wife and being very loving in his conversation to her, but this only deepened his wife's suspicions. Now the problem is in the hands of a good marriage-counseling clinic to which Mrs. Blank went at her husband's request, but very unwillingly. She is making a little progress. We only hope that her attitude can be changed before little Beatrice's personality is too much damaged and her future life jeopardized.

More seriously, the husband may be disabled by an accident, perhaps resulting in blindness, or hopelessly incapacitated by some chronic disease, arthritis, tuberculosis, cancer, paralysis, etc. Often the money received from the State is not sufficient and the wife has to work to supplement the income; or the husband, through no fault of his own may not be able to find sufficiently remunerative work.

Illustrating this observation, we have in mind two situations. The first may be told briefly, since even though the husband's condition is much more serious than in the second instance, it deals with a happy family. The family consists of George, the husband, thirty-five years old, who has a hopelessly chronic muscular neurological disease, painless but increasingly disabling; Mabel his wife, thirty years old, cheerful and efficient, and earning good wages as a hostess; baby Jack, two years old, and Mabel, Jr. an intelligent thirteen-year-old girl—a little gem. The mother has worked out a very good arrangement. Before she goes to work she gets breakfast for the children and sees Mabel, Jr. off to school. A kind neighbor comes in a few hours each day and for a small sum looks after the baby, supplementing what the husband can do. Little Mabel dashes home from school and is a marvelous little housekeeper. She is full of fun, too, now and then a trifle mischievous—a source of amusement, rather than trouble. Somehow the mother, with the wonderful alchemy of true motherhood sees to it that her daughter does not miss out on the pleasures and activities of girlhood. Occasionally she has her playmates in for a little party. The family have their pleasures—television, now and then the movies, visiting neighbors and having them call, etc. The mother by unanimous choice of the neighbors is always in charge of the annual neighborhood "porch party."

It is sad to turn to Mrs. J. She is forty years old. Her husband, forty-four, has fairly severe arthritis. He is not bedridden, but the arthritis is painful, and is not responding well to treatment as yet and there is not much he can do. The mother is employed as a secretary and earns a fairly good salary. There is one daughter, Mary, fourteen years old, a sullen, unhappy girl. She told a neighbor that she hates to see her mother coming home from work. Nine times out of ten, her mother will scold her and sometimes slap her for not having done all the chores she was told to do or for having stayed after school to play or for asking for a little spending money. "And don't bring those noisy girl friends of yours into the house. What with your father and all the other things I have to do, I am entitled to a little peace and quiet." Occasionally, no doubt feeling guilty and remorseful, Mary's mother kisses and hugs her. But these are only brief interludes and soon the old record of irritability and complaints is turned on again. Her husband, too, dreads his wife's homecoming. Everything she does for him is done with great effort and "patient resignation." "I am so tired I don't see how I can go on." Mrs. J.'s neighbors dislike her and have as little to do with her as possible. She is disagreeable and quarrels with them. We agree with Mrs. J. about one thing. As far as Mary is concerned we, too, do not see how it can go on much longer. Each week, indeed, each day, appreciably lessens Mary's chances of happiness and adjustment in marriage, as a mother, or in any other situation in life.

Wars—the United States having been engaged in three in a little more than twenty-five years—have taken a heavy toll and left many young women widows with young children. Sometimes the father has never seen his daughter or son. The young widow has a difficult problem to solve. It is not only the problem of death with the emotional deprivation it entails for children and possibly the economic necessity of earning a living for herself and her children. And the psychological tightrope-walking feat of being both mother and father. These considerations are discussed elsewhere in this book. But war-made widows have an additional hazard. What thoughts and remembrances of the father shall they leave in the minds of their children, particularly their daughters? They may think the kindest way is to say little or nothing, hoping the children will forget. They will not forget. As they grow older, questions, often stimulated by their playmates, will shape in their minds. If left unanswered, a hazardous psychological vacuum will occur. Some women create a beautiful, but somewhat overidealized and idolized figure of the father who gave his life for his country. This carries a risk. It may erect a roadblock of father hero worship in the emotional life of a girl, so that she will never be able to give her whole heart to another man. Or if the widow marries again the daughter may feel and display a deep hostility toward the stepfather, which not only beclouds her girlhood happiness and maturing but endangers her emotional future. There is a middle-of-the-road technique which is good. It is halfway between forgeting and idolizing. Perhaps it can be built from the attitude of "Your father was a fine, good, brave man and you can be proud to be his daughter."

We have presented several more or less irreversible situations in which the mother has to function in a dual mother-father capacity. We have emphasized that it is difficult.

What can and should be done? It is worth repeating the advice that these mothers should preserve their femininity and display it in the home. Do not become a feminist. Children recoil from masculinity in a mother, in dress or attitude. Or daughters may imitate it, which puts their future emotional life in jeopardy. Do not hesitate to use buttons and bows and all the embellishments of your sex. You may have to be cool and brisk in the business world, but in the home with the youngsters, let your temperature go up and resume the natural psychological curves of your sex. You may be fortunate enough to have a son in his teens. Lean on him a bit. Ask the girls for advice. If your husband is away, tell the youngsters to write to him and talk to him on the phone now and then. Tell them about his work.

You may have to do some homework in the evenings. If so, do it quietly and unobtrusively. Do not boast about your accomplishments in an exhibitionistic way. Tell of them modestly. Probably the girls will be more interested in a description of the "cute little blue rosette" on the shoulder strap of the dress than they will be in hearing how you beat your competitors to it and bought the whole output of dresses that will "sell like hot cakes from coast to coast."

Among the blocks to the achievement of motherhood and one which is often not inevitable, we give priority to divorce. Apparently divorce is often a mistake. Divorce always hurts children, particularly girls. Frequently it does irreparable harm. Almost always it psychologically beclouds their futures.

Sometimes, of course, divorce is mandatory. Scarcely, however, in the proportion which obtains in this country. Our divorce rate is shamefully larger than that of any other nation in the world.

We know some divorced women who do a masterly job and tell their daughters (and their sons) the best possible things about their fathers. They even stretch the truth a little. But there are not enough such women. With immature mothers it often gets to be a sordid affair. Sometimes incredibly so. Sighs and tears, often obvious bids for sympathy. Detailed descriptions of the brutal behavior of "that heel, lower than a worm, your father; and all his damn family."

Don't these women see what they are doing to their young daughters? Whether or not they are "heels," fathers will be the first loved and male heroes of their daughters. So the girl's emotional loyalties are subjected to terrific pressures and her personality is distorted. Often the divorced wife's tirades do not stop with her husband, but damn all males. The daughter is expected not only to disown her father, but to distrust all men. The chance of happiness in her future marriage is discounted in advance. And for that matter, so are her chances for real, mature satisfaction in life, married or not. No matter where she lives and what she does, she will always come into contact with men.

Mr. and Mrs. O. were unhappily married for ten years, then separated for a year and then divorced. The divorce libel gave the usual grounds—"cruel and barbarous treatment." A more truthful statement would have been: "We are both selfish. We are unwilling to meet the responsibilities of marriage or make any concessions and we don't like each other." There is a beautiful daughter, Nancy, now seventeen years old. The divorce gave the father visitation privileges but his visits were made so unpleasant that he ceased making them. Nancy now visits him twice a week.

Here is a report of the usual kind of interview Nancy has with her mother after she returns from a visit with her father. We said "interview." It really is not that. Nancy says very little. Her mother does the talking: "Well, you saw him. I suppose he told you how awful I was and warned you about me. I guess he made a big fuss over you, told you how pretty you are and how much he loves you. I think he just wants to wean you away from me. Was that old witch, his mother, there? Watch out for her. She's a troublemaker. And I guess that wonderful sister of his was on hand and made some snidish remarks about me. Nancy, the less you have to do with any of that tribe, the better off you will be." And so on.

Nancy is now under the care of a psychiatrist. Some

progress is being made but she is still stuck at this level: "Jim" [her boy friend] "is nice. I like him and he likes me. He wants me to marry him. But I am afraid to even think of marriage. It can be terrible."

If women asked us about divorce, we would say:

1. Don't get a divorce unless you feel there is no other way.

2. Even if you do decide there is no other way, still wait a reasonable time, especially if there are children. The situation may change.

3. Analyze your motives for getting a divorce. The more the reasons are *outside* the home—for instance, being in love with another man—the less reason for going ahead.

4. If you are a real mother, the effect of a divorce on the children should outweigh many other considerations.

5. If you do get a divorce, give your ex-husband as good a character as you possibly can to your children. The most helpful thing you can say to your daughter is: "It didn't work out for your father and me, but that is no reason to think you won't have a happy marriage. I believe you will."

Sometimes divorce results in odd twists. A woman, whose divorce was justified, remarried. She was meticulous in seeing that her daughter visited her father every two weeks, which was his legal right. The girl came home from these visits in a state of anxiety. The mother discovered that the father's new wife frequently warned the girl that her stepfather was a dangerous fellow who would probably try to rape her.

An extramarital love affair may interpose a barrier to the fulfillment of the mother function. The mother of three children came to us in a state of anxiety, depression and guilt, because she "hated the middle one," a girl, even finding it repugnant to touch her (she was a good mother to the other two children). She did not know why. A little probing brought out the fact that just before she became pregnant by her husband with this child, she had decided to seek a divorce and marry her lover. She felt the pregnancy barred this. So unconsciously the middle child became the symbol of failure to accomplish her objective and, as she believed, to find happiness.

What about sexual infidelity? Even if it is only one third as common in women as Kinsey suggests, it is still very important personally and socially. Modern so-called advanced thinking tends to condone it. Conversely, many people regard the sexually unfaithful wife as outside the pale, who should be branded as a harlot.

Jesus did not condone adultery, but we think in His love and mercy, He did understand it. The scribes and Pharisees in order to test His adherence to the ancient law, brought to Him a woman taken in adultery. He looked up at them and said, "He that is without sin among you, let him first cast a stone at her."

Those who were about to stone her to death, departed.

Jesus spoke gently to the woman, "Neither will I condemn thee. Go, and now sin no more."

We are not writing an eternal-triangle book. We are chiefly interested at this point in what happens to the children and particularly the daughters of wives who break their marriage vows. It is no use pretending that marital infidelity of mothers does not harm their daughters. It does. Some women rationalize, perhaps quite sincerely:

"If I have no love life at all, I will lose all animation and feeling. Then I will be bad for my children. My daughters will feel marriage is a snare and a delusion." Sometimes the effort to guard the secret extramarital affairs succeeds. "What they don't see can't hurt them." More likely than not, something leaks out from the home behavior of the woman who is in love, but not with her husband. That "something" may be enough to make her daughter cynical about marriage or even to pave the way to imitate her mother in her own marriage. Some very immature, harebrained women are so moved by the "grand passion" (which is usually a puerile, sickly affair) that they desert their children and embark on the great love adventure. Others seek divorce. Many more women, even though deeply in love, place their children first and manage, somehow or other, to muddle through.

Since we dealt with the problem and perhaps helped to untangle its complications we know that the very attractive and intelligent Mrs. W., who was having an extramarital love affair, nevertheless loved her fourteen-year-old daughter Catherine deeply and Catherine loved her just as much. We will never know surely whether or not Catherine knew about her mother's love affair. Certainly she sensed something was not right.

Mrs. W.'s husband was a quiet, undemonstrative man, rather colorless but in his way devoted to his wife and daughter. Catherine loved him. Mr. and Mrs. W. did not get on well sexually and by mutual consent they had ceased their sex life. It would fit in nicely to say that Mrs. W.'s lover was a scoundrel. He was not. He was deeply in love with Mrs. W. but was also deeply troubled by the situation. They talked of divorce but decided that would hurt Catherine too much. So they went on muddling through somehow.

Catherine and her mother were very close and the child was very intelligent and observant. We have little doubt that she saw through the show of affection her mother showed for her father when she was present. And, one time when Catherine's mother returned from seeing her lover, Catherine said, "You look so happy, Mother. Where do you go that makes you so happy? You never take me."

Though they loved each other the extramarital love affair was scarcely happy. It had to be clandestine. There was always the danger of discovery. And Catherine was not herself. So these two people with the help of a psychiatrist brought the affair to a conclusion. Mrs. W. does a fairly good job with her husband and finds much compensation in Catherine who again is a happy child.

This has not been an easy chapter to write. Some of the obstacles in the way of attaining successful motherhood are indeed high and formidable. Some cannot be overcome. Some of the obstacles are made by neglectful mothers, usually unconsciously, occasionally it would seem to be with almost wilful deliberation. Many of the problems are in an intermediate territory— "Perhaps something more could have been done about it," but again, "Perhaps not." Often one may say, "Judge not, that you may not be judged." Women are often caught in the grinding cogs of life and cannot extricate themselves.

Chapter V

NOT ONLY death but many other situations make it mandatory for children to have mother surrogates. The mother may be so hopelessly sick physically that she cannot function at all. She may be mentally sick and in a mental hospital. She may be delinquent or even criminal and in prison. Occasionally in a divorce suit the mother's behavior has been such that the judge denies her custody of her children. And there are other reasons for surrogates.

Then, too, as children grow older and their lives expand they find partial mother surrogates, such as schoolteachers, and later on even college professors. And, of course, relatives and friends.

Let us picture a not too uncommon tragedy. A mother dies, or for some other reason—perhaps incurable mental disease—can no longer care for her two daughters four and seven years old. The father is so situated that he cannot look after them. Then, in the first place, there may be a battle between the mother's and father's relatives as to who is to have the little girls, both sides of the family wanting them. On the other hand, no one may really want them but finally someone may take them through a sense of duty. How destructive this may be is illustrated by the case of Ruth as given in the chapter, "The Childhood Vacuum."

But let us suppose that everyone, grandparents, aunts, sisters, friends, want to take the two lovely little girls, deprived of their mother, into their hearts and homes. The grandparents may not be young enough—in fact they may be old and crotchety. At first they may be very enthusiastic about having the girls, but as time goes on they begin to be irritated by the activity and noise of the children. They do not understand children two generations removed from their own childhood. Or they may simply dote on "poor Margaret's little angels," give them everything they want including their own way and spoil them hopelessly. When the children are welcomed by aunts or sisters who may be married and have children of their own, we have seen two kinds of problems arise. In one, the surrogate sister or aunt gradually begins to favor her own children and discriminate against the two little girls. Occasionally this may involve actual cruelty as it did in the case of Ruth. Surprisingly often we have seen the opposite, the children of the sister or aunt made to give way and concede to the two "poor little chicks who have lost their mother." Of course, this produces rivalry and friction between the children and unhappiness in the home. It takes as much love and skill to be a good surrogate mother as it does to be a flesh-and-blood mother, maybe more. Several times we have observed the adoption of motherless daughters by close friends, who were childless, work out splendidly. The children, sometimes old enough to re-member "Aunt Jennie," their mother's dearest friend, have really found a good mother.

Many years ago, one of the authors knew this situation very intimately. A splendid mother died in the child-birth of her third daughter. Her husband, a professional man, struggled along for a year trying to look after his three little daughters with the help of inadequate house-keepers. It was a dismal failure. Then Winifred, who had been deeply in love with the man before he married her most dear friend Agnes, and who had never married, asked if she could have the children. He agreed. She did a beautiful job for the children. It was compensation for her lost love. The father of the children and Winifred are now both dead. But Winifred lived long enough to see the three children happily married and to hold and love many "grandchildren."

A governess may often be almost reverently spoken of as "a veritable gem." Her competance is unchallenged. When company comes, Mademoiselle discretely herds her angelic charges into the upper reaches of the house. The mother is delighted; Mademoiselle quietly and efficiently takes care of "everything." Therein lies the very heart of the problem. For Mademoiselle is too quiet and efficient —too perfect.

But she is not quite so retiring with the children. She may be starved for love and affection. She has never been given the opportunity to satisfy her natural desires for companionship and the love of others. She tries to find what life has denied her. Young girls are more likely to succumb to her. Gently, but treacherously in so far as the lives of these girls are concerned, she engulfs great segments of their emotional lives and makes them her own. Literally and figuratively, she "takes over" the minds and bodies of these children. She is in a position to channel and oversee their actions and reactions. *The girls become her daughters.* But she is not married to their father; she is still only the governess. She can be little more than a proxy mother, and this is not sufficient to produce a well-adjusted adult. After all, Mademoiselle is not, and cannot be, the mother.

The emotional areas which should be watched over by the mothers themselves, and which this governess appropriates for herself, are often lost forever. Only within the past few months has a young mother of two children been capable of conversing with any degree of ease with her mother, or indeed with anyone else in her family. She could not even begin to listen to advice or counsel of any kind. In the mirror of her psyche her old governess would appear and still any feeble attempts to communicate with her family. She still, by the way, clucks her tongue when emotionally upset, much as "Nannie" used to do.

We hope that not many mothers who read this book have to have governesses for their children. Wealth is not a good enough reason. An efficient governess is a temptation for the mother to spend less and less time with the children. Of course, there may be circumstances which make it necessary to employ a governess. If so, be sure she is a trustworthy, mature woman. And spend as much time with your children as you possibly can.

Many mothers and fathers are entirely too casual about baby-sitters. Sometimes very horrible things happen:

Theft, abduction, cruelty to the children, sexual indecencies. There may be complete indifference in looking after the children—sitting in another room and reading and never going near them. There have been instances where children have been hurt or where some illness suddenly appeared. Sometimes baby-sitters may invite in their boy friends and have a rollicking time, beer drinking, dancing, necking. It is not too difficult to find out about the baby-sitters you may employ. The majority of them are reliable. But be sure. Investigate their references. Are they sponsored by a community organization? Do you know their families? What has been the experience of your friends with them?

We find occasionally spinsters among trained nurses—women whom life has cheated emotionally. They leave nothing to be desired in bringing children through grave illnesses with skill, devotion and tenderness. But here the danger arises that the nurse may cleave too tightly to the child; when their patient has recovered and they leave, they may well take with them an irreplaceable part of the child. Many nurses will care only for children. Most of these are emotionally mature women who perform their duties admirably, both professionally and personally. A few, of equal professional ability, are frustrated in their own lives and emotionally immature. The damage they do, stemming from their own inadequate lives, does much, we fear, to cancel out the physical recovery that has been made through their professional skill.

Again we feel the hazard is greater for little girls than for boys. The illness is apt to occur at an age when the transference to a mother substitute is very easy. Sickness provides a bridge. It increases the helplessness and insecurity of the child and it reaches out lovingly to the one who helps. Much of this is good, but it can go too far. The mother, of course, without interfering with the functions and duties of the nurse, should keep close contact with her sick child and by her calm, loving conduct demonstrate that *she* is the *mother* in whom there is to be found supreme love, confidence, and security.

At least one half of a child's waking life is spent in contact, direct and indirect, with her schoolteacher. Naturally, among the great body of schoolteachers, there are many—intellectually capable, perhaps honor students at teachers' college—who are not emotionally equipped to cope with the teaching of children. Children learn a great deal in school that falls outside the realm of formal instruction. Far more important are the emotional lessons. The indispensable lesson to be learned does not lie in mastery of the multiplication tables or memorization of the state capitals, but rather in a capacity to understand the give-and-take basis on which the mature life is founded. Life is lived largely not by the intellect, but by maturely motivated emotions. This is doubly true for girls. In very intimate fashion they will deal in their future lives with emotional problems of husbands and children. To achieve effectively the needs imposed by adult life, intellectual development and emotional growth must attain a minimal level. Although intellectual measurements can be increased over a period of time (unless especially deficient), the emotional status cannot, by the mere process of addition, improve itself overnight. The emotional development of a child's personality can only take place at specific times over a period of years. Otherwise the whole structure of the personality will lack support, and it will crumble of its own weight in the face of demands put on it by adverse occurrences in the emotional and social life of the adult world. It is no exaggeration to say that any person who comes frequently in contact with children either adds something to or detracts something from a child's process of maturing. The personality keeps a record of everything. Nothing is omitted from the final tally of joy and unhappiness. Schoolteachers are much like the rest of us—some mature, some immature. A child cannot receive more than the teacher has to give. Especially, the teacher cannot give more to the children of her own sex. Given such intimate contact, the chances to help or hinder are virtually limitless.

Most schoolteachers are not married. In some communities single teachers are preferred to married ones, regardless of their other qualifications. Many teachers are no longer young. If a teacher falls into the "old maid" category, that is no reason to fear a damaging influence on the emotional development of the children who come into her classes. We know many spinster teachers who face life with a healthy, mature outlook. They have learned to understand and accept their particular barriers of frustration. There has resulted a mellowing of their characters and an insight which is often broader and more mature than the viewpoints of many who have known a personal emotional relationship in marriage.

Some teachers have kept honor rolls of their pupils in school—men and women who have gained fame, but more important, men and women who are leading lives of high emotional and social maturity. These include wives and mothers, husbands and fathers, as well as citizens who daily contribute something of themselves to their community. To any good mother, women teachers of this type are vital allies. Their tempering influence, brought about by viewpoints stressed in the school environment, may often suffice to overcome the detrimental effects produced on a child by an immature mother. Much has been said about the dangers of the emotional attachments teen-age girls may form to the women teachers. In some instances this is true enough. But there are many emotional attachments which are healthy and growth-promoting rather than hindering.

A teacher (perhaps, particularly a spinster) can be the wrong kind of surrogate mother—a mom in the worst sense of the word. She transfers the outpourings of her own frustrations and emotional sufferings onto the heads of the children under her control. In this, at least, she deprives them of nothing. If her personality has taken a sadistic turn, she is capable of doling out a form of pain far more penetrating than if she were permitted to employ corporal punishment. She has all the tools for inflicting mental pain —the whips of unbending authority, arbitrary discipline, "clever" sarcasm and the humiliation of the child before her friends. A poor girl from the "wrong side of the tracks" may be ten minutes late for school, because she helped her mother get breakfast for the younger children. The sadistic teacher may inform the class: "Mary is late again. I'm afraid she spent too much time with her rouge and lipstick." What this woman is really telling the children is this: I hate and resent you. You will pay for the children I could not have. I shall do everything in my power to prevent your being happy wives and husbands, mothers and fathers. You shall not have those things which I was denied."

Usually a woman of this sort will have one or more favorites in the class. These children's faults are quickly overlooked. As far as they are concerned, anything goes. Apparently there are a few remains of mothering that cannot be suppressed even in these embittered women. With the other children, however, the pets are apt to pay through the nose for the teacher's attention.

On the other hand, we may find a teacher who is as saintly as her opposite number is sinful. She adores the children and is blindly sentimental in all her dealings with them. Discipline never enters her head. "They're really just babies." She has a whole battery of ready-made excuses for the failings of "her" children. She passes these out wholesale to teachers, parents and principal alike.

Either of these extremes in teachers is detrimental to any mother who is trying to help her child through the many mazes on the road to maturity. The strict teacher fills the path with the stumbling blocks of stubbornness and the rankling sense of indiscriminate justice and resentment. The doting teacher gives out so much ice cream and cake that the child is quite lost when she tries to establish a foothold in the give-and-take world. If the child has an immature mother, she is faced with a double barrier in her struggle for maturity—one at school, the other at home.

Advice to mothers about teachers: get to know the teacher as a person and, if possible, establish friendly relations with her. Tactfully try to gain some idea of her attitudes, but do not pry into her private life. If your daughters wish to discuss their teachers with you, do so, but do not let the discussion get out of hand. Often children are not very discriminating and their appraisal of the teacher may be idealistically admiring or unrealistically damning. Be *sure* before you decide your daughter is being discriminated against and being treated unfairly by the teacher. Usually you will be wrong. If the situation does not seem quite serious, do not gird yourself for action and do battle with the teacher. Talk it over quietly with her. Parent-teacher groups, if well organized and well run, are excellent forums of contact between mothers and teachers. Mutual understanding develops. In these and other ways, the teacher collaborates with the mother in producing something more important than a textbook can produce—an intelligent and emotionally grown-up young woman, who in her future life will be responsible and responsive in any situation she may be called upon to meet.

We repeat that if there seems to be friction and difficulty between your daughter and her teacher do not make a spur-of-the-moment decision that your child is entirely innocent and the teacher unfair and report her to the school authorities. Sometimes it is a good idea to invite the teacher to your home for dinner and in a comfortable, relaxed atmosphere after dinner talk over the problem.

Mrs. Jones' little Patricia, thirteen years old, complained bitterly about her teacher. Miss Higginsbottom was mean to her, found fault with her schoolwork, kept her after school, scolded her in front of the other children, "made fun" of her, etc. At first Mrs. Jones was indignant and ready to report the teacher to the Board of Education. But then she thought it over and decided instead to invite her to dinner. Miss Higginsbottom proved to be a young, rather attractive woman, a recent college graduate with a somewhat flustered, embarrassed manner. The dinner conversation with Patricia at the table was a bit strained and after dinner she and Mrs. Jones talked things over.

It appeared that a considerable part of the difficulty was due to Patricia. "I make fun of her?" exclaimed Miss H. indignantly, "Why, Mrs. Jones, Pat makes fun of me. When my back is turned she makes faces and tries to imitate me before the other girls. Once, I intercepted a note she was passing to another girl [here the teacher stammered and blushed] which read "Miss Higgins-bottom is fat." Mrs. Jones said, "That was very mean of Pat. What did you do?" A longer pause then with an outburst of frankness, Miss H. said: "Well, Mrs. Jones, I guess it's at least partly my fault. I just got mad and stayed mad. And I tried to make things tough for Pat. I should not have done that. I should have talked it out with Pat. I'm sure it would have worked out. I like Pat and I think underneath she really likes me." Then a long pause and several sighs. "I have no right to bother you with my personal affairs but you are older than I am and you seem nice and understanding. I have been having trouble with my boy friend and I guess I am edgy."

Neither the teacher nor Mrs. Jones punished Pat. Her mother did have a heart-to-heart talk with her. Mrs. Jones and Miss H. become firm friends. As time went on, Pat, too, would talk things over with her mother and her teacher. Pat became a proponent for Miss H. At her own initiative at Christmas, Pat became chairman of the committee to buy Miss H. a gift and she gave it to her, making a lovely little presentation speech.

As we look back over our many participations in mother-teacher frictions, sometimes officially, a clear line of cleavage emerges. It separates reasonably mature from decidedly immature mothers. Of course, the mature mothers make some mistakes, but usually they deal with teacher-daughter problems wisely and diplomatically. In the eyes of immature mothers who are possessive, their daughters are always right, their teachers are always wrong and "terrible." Many immature mothers go far beyond their own daughters. They may want certain girls removed from school because they are "a bad influence on my darling." "Why does my Mary Jane have to sit next to Susie?" (A poor girl from the slums.) "Why can't she sit next to Constantine?" (Whose father is rich and influential.) "Don't you dare teach my innocent little baby those dirty things about sex!" The innocent little baby was fifteen years old and quite sophisticated. In one school where we helped plan a course of instruction for girls on the art and artistry of being a good wife and mother, the moms banded together and raised such a protest that the course had to be abandoned. They could not take the implied criticism of themselves.

Not all mother surrogates are of flesh and blood. There are surrogates of brick and mortar, representing rather feeble social efforts to supply the mother need. These we treat in the next chapter.

Chapter VI

CIVILIZATIONS OF the future will not tolerate orphan asylums. In our very prejudiced opinion, orphan asylums are still gray, drab, gloomy places.

One of the authors remembers as a little boy walking with his parents one Sunday morning and passing an orphan asylum. He asked what it was. His parents explained about orphans. It was more than fifty years ago, but still vividly remembered is the sudden clutch of fear at the little boy's heart, the tightening of his clasp on his parents' hands and his frantic attempt to hurry them away from the building.

This is not quite fair. Now, many of these institutions are modern in construction, with bright and inviting façades. More importantly, some of them are built on the cottage plan, each cottage being in charge of a house-mother. Some of these women are kind and sympathetic —all in all, rather good mother surrogates. But too many of these institutions are still gray and forbidding, often quite hygienic and sanitary, but chillingly impersonal.

Even though the treatment is good and kind in a "home" yet the effect is always uncertain. Particularly is this true if the child as it grows up has reason to suspect that it is illegitimate.

Margery B. is thirty-six years old. She is now happily married to an engineer and has two little girls, six and eight years old. But the first eight years of her ten years of married life were miserably unhappy. As a few-weeks-old infant she was left on the doorstep of a Catholic foundling home. The sisters took her in and raised her. As she grew older she began to ask about her parents and whether she was illegitimate. The sisters had nothing to tell her. She got on well with them and helped with the work. At the age of twenty she entered the sisterhood as a novitiate. After several years she became dissatisfied and with the advice and good wishes of the sisters left the order and the home. While working as a file clerk she met a young engineer. They fell in love and married. Then the trouble began.

In spite of the fact that her husband made a good salary and was able to give her a very nice home she was miserably unhappy. She felt he was "uppish" and referred too often to his family, which he rarely did. When his mother stopped in she was rude to her. His only other living relative, a sister, liked Margery and loved the children but Margery was unpleasant to her— "She's always hinting that I'm a bastard." If the children even vaguely asked an innocent question about her family or said anything nice about "Granny" or "Aunt Nora" she would burst into tears, retire to her room and sulk for hours. She even felt that the ladies in the bridge club purposely boasted about their families in order to shame her, and that the grocery boy looked askance at her. The situation became intolerable. Finally her husband persuaded her to talk things over with him and they had several heart-to-heart talks. In effect he said to her, "Margery, I love you. I don't give a damn who your parents were. They were probably good people who got caught in a jam. Let's forget it and live for each other. If you have to say anything just say your mother and father were killed in an accident when you were a baby." This attitude, plus a very few interviews with a sensible psychiatrist, straightened things out and Margery began to find real happiness with her husband and children. Nevertheless, if the questions, "Who was my mother? Who was my father?" cannot be answered, there is left an emotional vacuum which is hard to fill.

Foster homes? They are good, bad and indifferent. It all depends on the foster mother and the family. In a good foster home, the foster mother creates a psychological décor of kindness, care and consideration. Often she is able to give love, perhaps particularly if she is childless. In the indifferent home, there may be satisfactory food and physical hygiene, but the atmosphere is bleakly impersonal. The bad foster home is really bad—often insufficient food, unkindness, sometimes cruelty, sometimes danger.

We can only give Sylvia R. a few paragraphs. She deserves a book. Sylvia is twenty-eight years old, married to a social worker and has two young children. During the past ten years her life has been a pattern of many depressive attacks, interspersed with severe anxiety attacks and many fears and compulsions. Often she is deeply preoccupied with suicidal thoughts. She thinks she would never have "the nerve" to take her life, but we are not so sure. When depressed, she is very self-reproachful: "I am a nasty woman. I neglect the children, sometimes don't even feed them. I am mean to my husband and I am always taking mean digs at him." The husband is a kind, even-tempered, unselfish, long-suffering man. Said Sylvia: "I don't know why I feel so hostile toward him." Then later, "I think I hate him because he is like Mother in so many ways."

Sylvia's mother died when she was eleven, her father when she was twelve. Her father's death was mysterious. There was some thought of homicide and she did not know he had died until a week later. One brother also died under strange circumstances, and Sylvia at the age of fifteen had to go to a distant city to identify his body in the morgue.

Sylvia felt her mother neither wanted her nor loved her. She could recall only a single happy time with her, one day when she came home from school and her mother put her arms around her. She remembered wishing it could be that way all the time. Of her mother's death she said, "I wasn't sorry when Mother died. I had made up my mind to take care of my father anyway, cook for him and keep house for him."

When she was a little girl she adored her father. "I don't know why I did. He was a weak character. He couldn't refuse liquor. He mourned Mother's death and went to pieces. He was only concerned about himself, not me."

Sylvia's sex life is woefully incomplete. She did not have any sexual relations with her husband during the first five months of marriage. An operation was performed to help the situation, but it did not. It was not until after three years of marriage that there was any kind of sexual relationship and it was not satisfactory. In fact, sex has never given her the least pleasure. She wanted the first baby to see if she could have one. She did not want the second child and resents it. Whatever chance there was of reasonably normal sex development was given the *coup de grâce* in three of the eleven foster homes in which Sylvia was farmed out between the ages of twelve and eighteen. She hated each foster home. Each one added to her store of hostility and her removal was usually requested because she was so "hateful." She had not had any preparation for her first menstrual period and her toilette was clumsy. The foster mother told her she was "a dirty girl." In another home the foster mother established quasi-friendly relations, but chiefly told her of the horrors of sexual life and how women had to submit to "this terrible thing." One night Sylvia stumbled upon this woman having relations with her husband and apparently enjoying it. This confused and frightened her. In another home the husband of the foster mother made sexual advances to her and tried to rape her. Only her struggles and screams saved her.

You will wonder why these things were not discovered by those who supervised and inspected the foster homes. Well, often supervision is a rather sketchy business. Furthermore, food and conditions can be inspected, but protection, consideration and love can be neither inspected nor commanded.

In treatment, Sylvia is making a fair amount of progress. Certain odds and ends coming to the surface from the unconscious would indicate that, in spite of the surface rejection of her parents, underneath Sylvia is dominated by a severe and overly rigid superego or conscience. Deep in her psyche the patient has accepted responsibility for the death of her parents and perhaps also her brother. There is strong guilt concerning the wish to get her mother out of the way. In a sense this was fulfilled, and the death of her father was her punishment for wishing to replace her mother with him. There is a tremendous longing for acceptance and love which was never given by the mother.

According to the ideology of the dictatorships, children owe their first allegiance and love to the state and they are so trained. From leaks through the iron curtain it would appear that children are encouraged to inform on their parents. It is a dangerous doctrine, dangerous for democracy, dangerous for the dictatorships. It might succeed in producing robots, but one day the robots may turn and rend the master which denied the expression of mother love. Of all surrogates for the mother, the state is the least satisfactory.

We hope we have not over-painted the picture and left the inference that loving parents will suffice and that all will be well in the future. True enough, mother and parental love in early life are bedrock, the foundation. Without them, it is most difficult to build a sound, enduring personality. But many things must be added to this foundation to produce a solid edifice. There is intelligence and reasoning and common sense, which is very uncommon. And there is the capacity to plan for the future. And there is the development of a code of ethics, a spirituality if you wish, which the child receives first from the mother and then modifies and expands as it grows older. With love alone and none of these things, the child would be defense-less in the face of the buffetings of life. But without love, it is not easy for these other qualities to come to full fruition.

Chapter VII

MOTHERS WHO NEVER GREW UP

It is unlikely that silver cords have any sex of their own. They can be affixed as firmly to the male as to the female offspring. We are here particularly interested in those which are fastened to female children by immature mothers. At first, and in certain phases of childhood, the reign of the mother over daughter is complete and her domination may be absolute.

There is the rather likeable, but nevertheless mistaken, mom—the "Manager"—who goes to no end of trouble in selecting for her daughters, well toward being grown up, their shoes and clothes, their hairdos, their companions, their extracurricular activities, their social attitudes and opinions. "Selecting" here does not mean wise guidance, but control: "We will do it this way." Only occasionally is the dominance unrelenting and arbitrary, with punishment following swiftly upon the heels of disregard of maternal orders: "You can't go to that party next Saturday," "No tennis this week," "No allowance until next week." More common is the technique of indirection, often soft, persuasive, devious. When mother is disobeyed, she is not angry. She is hurt and sad and the tears start from her eyes. And the daughter feels guilty. The soft method is infinitely more successful than the tough one in blocking manifestations of youthful independence of thinking and acting.

A girl of fifteen, shopping with her mother, fixed her eyes and heart upon one of the dresses. Perhaps it was not the wisest selection in the shop, but it was inexpensive and serviceable. Said mother: "Of course, if you insist, darling, you can have it, but I know you won't be as happy with it as you would be with that lovely gray one and I would be just a wee bit disappointed (sigh). I gave up my bridge to come with you and help you get just the nicest dress (deep sigh)." Joan "decided" on the gray dress.

The real mother uses a compound of common sense and love in bringing up her children. As they grow, she makes an effort to lead them to think independently. She knows that in questions of selection—whether of clothes or of beliefs—careful guidance is essential, but she also knows that this guidance should be meted out in ever-decreasing doses as her child progresses toward the ultimate goal of independent decision. She cannot allow a daughter in her early teens to wear a very sophisticated evening gown to her first "formal." Nor can she give into her daughter's overwhelming desire for the black-lace underthings she has seen in a magazine.

After all, clothes and hairdos in themselves are not of paramount importance, except as symbols. It is important—unfair indeed—when "momistic" thinking is inflicted on the opinions and attitudes of the adolescent, because this technique is based, not on explanation and discussion, but on smoke-screening and clouding of issues. Moms discourage (often unknowingly) self-reliance in the views and opinions of their children. Whether the opinions are right or not is of little consequence; what matters is that they are signal-flag warnings that the son or daughter is gradually switching away from the maternal track. So mom stifles any indications of maturing thought and emotion. She may not realize what she is doing, but the effect on the children is just as damaging as if she did it deliberately.

We think that particularly at this time is it dangerous to "possess" the thinking of children. More than ever before are we living not only in an imperiled world, but in a changing one. It seems possible that in the growth principle inherent in each child, there are at least some vague stirrings which respond to environmental changes. This trend had better not be blocked. Mothers have no crystal globes. They cannot possibly foresee the kind of lives their sons and daughters will have to live and the new conditions they will encounter. It seems more than likely that the children of today will live in a world in which evil ideologies will strive with even greater intensity than they do now to enslave men's minds, and those who have never learned to think for themselves will be easy victims.

"You may give them your love, but not your thoughts,
   For they have their own thoughts.
   You may house their bodies, but not their souls,
   For their souls dwell in the house of tomorrow, which
   You cannot visit, even in your dreams." *

* Reprinted from THE PROPHET by Kahlil Gibran with permission of the publisher, Alfred A. Knopf, Inc. Copyright 1923 by Kahlil Gibran; renewal copyright 1951 by Administrators C.T.A. of Kahlil Gibran Estate, and Mary G. Gibran.

The authors of this book, whose reservoirs of energy are not inexhaustible, are amazed and admiring in our contemplation of the "No Trouble" mother. She may look tired, and often feels so, but rarely will she admit it. Yet our admiration must be tinctured with regret that the cause she serves so faithfully is a mistaken one. Actually she cares little about herself. Her joy in life lies in serving her children. From sunup to sunset she finds complete satisfaction in waiting on her children hand and foot. The house is theirs. Everything must be just right. Mealtime is set by the children; "favorite" dishes are the order of the day every day. The children need never stop on the way home for a bite, for the refrigerator is always well stocked with snacks mother has prepared for just such an emergency. Even late at night the sound of the key in the front door is apt to be the cue for mom to call gently, "Kids, you'll find milk and sandwiches in the icebox. Would you like me to come down and make you a hot snack?" There is never any need to worry about that missing button or that misplaced sweater in this house. Mother will fix it, or mother will find it. "Let me get it for you," is one of her favorite expressions. With joy in her heart she follows the wake of her children who have littered every corner of the house with their belongings. She covers literally miles a day in pursuit of stray articles. Her reward is her service.

The No Trouble mother is somewhat more likely to serve her sons than her daughters. However, we have encountered many who "picked up" after their daughters just as eagerly. "Dear little Jane. After all she is still a child, only sixteen years old. She has so much to do, what with her lessons, the glee club, her girl friends and the boys. You know Jane is very popular. I say, let her have fun now. She can learn later on." And Jane almost never does learn.

Even though Jane is somewhat selfish, yet she is attractive and good-natured, so probably she will marry. Then there will be trouble. It is unlikely that she will wed a young man who will be willing to clean up after her, unless it be at times of household emergencies, when all hands turn to. It is not unlikely that her husband will expect Jane to look after *his* shirts and socks and what not. It will be rather worse if Jane marries a young man who likes to pick up her scattered clothes and do the dishes and put them away. Rather worse, since if he is that kind of a young man, then the chances are he will lack certain other masculine traits which Jane will miss. Of course, they can compromise by living in a pigpen.

We have visited a few pigpen houses. No, they were not in the slums. They were the houses of people in the upper-middle brackets, costing $25,000 to $30,000 each. Usually there was one maid. One such house is presided over by a young woman, a college graduate, who has a distinguished cultural background. She can converse interestingly about the topics of the day, but we do not profit much, since our attention is distracted by the aroma of unwashed diapers and the problem of getting across the living room without tripping over the litter.

This young woman is one of three daughters of an affluent family. All through their childhoods their mother "saved" them and "did" for them. She does even now when they are married and have children of their own.

Not only is the mother a No Trouble mother, but she has a very high place on the list of mothers who are total failures. The marriages of the two other daughters are on the rocks. The marriage of the one we discussed is in serious jeopardy.

Kitty is a pretty, amiable, twenty-year-old unmarried girl. She gets on well with people, until she tries to live with them. Both for economic and social reasons, she would like to share an apartment with other girls from the office and has tried it several times. It never works out. One of these girls divulged this: "Kitty is a nice kid, but she is impossible to live with. To say she is not neat and has no sense of order is putting it very mildly. We are not paragons of neatness, but we like to live half decently. Kitty just wouldn't do her share of the work, even in her own room. We had to clean it and pick up her things all over the apartment. If Kitty cooked a meal, which was seldom, it was more trouble than it was worth. It took us a long time to find the dish cloths and towels and wash the dishes and put them away. So, tactfully as we could, we asked Kitty to make another arrangement."

We like to think that the first cave woman straightened the animal skins on the floor, which the men had kicked around, and even hung one or two on the walls of the cave for adornment.

The lesson is obvious. Every mother by example and teaching should inculcate into the personalities of her daughters at least a minimal standard of cleanliness, neatness and orderliness. Enough, but not too much. Over-fastidiousness is not a virtue. One woman counts the sheets returned from the laundry a dozen times and is still not satisfied it is the right count. Another is distressed and made miserable by a speck of dust on the floor or a spot on a dress so small that it is scarcely visible to the naked eye. These women are obsessive and compulsive. They are sick with a neurosis no mother would want to inflict on her daughters.

We have to descend several rungs on the ladder of emotional maturity to view the professionally "Frail" mother. She harms her daughters seriously, and, indeed, belongs to the life-wrecking crew of moms.

This is the mother who has given "all her strength" in bearing her children. Usually she is in middle life and pitifully weak; she just hasn't the strength to raise a finger, especially in the morning. Medical science can find no trace of organic disease. "Your mother isn't very strong." Of course, this mother never breathes a word about her plight. Nevertheless, the state of her health is common knowledge to everyone, including the delivery boy. Needless to say, her children always know. This mom casts her net wide and deep. Occasionally she nets a son. More often the catch is a daughter, whose heart is filled with loving pity for her invalid mother. The silver cord is tightly drawn and securely knotted around this daughter. If one could look behind the portals of this mother's conscious mind, her unconscious would say, "Why not? Giving all for me should give you great happiness. Didn't I give all for you in bringing you into the world, and didn't I use all the strength I had left in protecting you and caring for you when you couldn't shift for yourself?"

Psychiatrists can see the rub. Mom is not playing fair. We would warn, "Let the buyer beware." We have seen too often how the death of an invalid mother can shatter the life of her daughters. They can no longer enter the give-and-take world. Successful marriage is no longer possible. Their wombs may be doomed to be barren. The silver cord has been drawn so tight that it has cut off all other threads of social and personal life. Behind the façade of devotion and self-sacrifice the murmurings of "what might have been," begin to make themselves heard. There is a stirring of the realization that a fraud has been committed which may well result in a flood of hatred and resentment against the memory of the mother. It may even pour out from the dim backwaters of repression. A woman who had been chained all her life by a selfish invalid mother, now herself gravely sick with a high fever, muttered in her dilirium, again and again, "That black cat who sucked away my life."

Selfish invalid-mother situations occur with alarming frequency in our practice. An attractive girl of nineteen works hard in an office all day to contribute to the family budget. In the family are her mother and father and an older brother who lives at home. Almost never can Elizabeth go out at night. If she does, mother is almost sure to have a "staring" attack, during which she moans and gazes about blindly. In these attacks mother cannot recognize anyone in the family—*only Elizabeth*. So if Elizabeth is out, she has to hurry home. The rare times she is out for a few hours, she phones home repeatedly to see if mom is all right.

A sensible friend told Elizabeth she must see a psychiatrist. She demurred. She would have to make an evening appointment. It would be difficult. Mother kept a close check. She would not want to deceive her own mother. She always told her where she would be. We suspect that Elizabeth is caught hook, line and sinker. She does not feel particularly "put upon." In fact, she feels guilty unless she is with mother at night. "Suppose she died and I was not with her?"

We reserve judgment about Elizabeth's mother. We hope she is not feigning. Perhaps it is a neurosis. Neuroses carry with them a secondary gain, which is some advantage gained by the neurotic from the illness. Psychiatrists scrutinize it with some professional suspicion. True enough, the neurosis is unconscious, but the secondary-gain motivation may partake of conscious deliberation.

Even if the daughter does marry, it does not necessarily solve the situation. Perhaps the frail mother lives with the young married couple. Or, if not, the series of sad complaints from the ailing mother, by letter and phone, may make the daughter feel so guilty and so deplete her morale that her marriage falls by the wayside.

While it does not give absolution to those selfish mothers who refuse to release their daughters, even though they may live at the ends of the earth, yet there is another side to the case. We would like to present it in order to promote a better understanding and appreciation of the tough job of being a good mother. It is seldom fully understood and appreciated by men, and strangely enough, equally seldom by mothers themselves.

Perhaps a comparison may be made between the "career" of being a mother and the career of a successful business or professional man. Adeptness in motherhood or in business or in a profession is not inherited. It is learned on the job by hard work. They both start equally. The woman has not yet had any babies, the man is looking for work. The man—often still a boy—begins his career on one of the lower rungs of the ladder. He works long and hard hours, usually in a menial and monotonous capacity—office, errand, or copy boy, helper in packaging goods, or what not. In medicine, he is a "pre-med," later a medical student, both rather underdogs. As an interne he is only a few barks ahead. In law he is a humble law clerk. And so on. All of these tyros have to establish good relations with the men they work with and their superiors—not always easy. However, if things go reasonably well, the man is more or less "set" in his career soon after middle age. His worst obstacles are behind him. He begins to enjoy the gratification and security of having a relatively important role in a smoothly running enterprise. Both his superiors and inferiors respect and like him. He can take it a little easier—an afternoon of golf now and then and afterward in the clubhouse the satisfaction of having his opinion listened to with respect and interest. The younger men will attend to the details of the work.

Let us flash back to the successful mother career. The girl marries and accepts a position of being a mother. She, too, can count on long, hard hours and plenty of menial and monotonous work. True enough, children and their development are fascinating. Sometimes less fascinating than other times. A mother is tied more closely to her career than a man. Three meals a day, cleaning, mending and tending are not always so fascinating. The same damn thing over and over again. Then there are the inevitable illnesses of children and often a few extra ones. The mother may be required to function not only as a housekeeper, but also as a day and night nurse. It is a labor of love, but love may be pretty exacting. The children grow older. Mother does not have a sinecure, but things are easier. Then suddenly the last bell tolls. The youngest daughter graduates from college or marries and leaves home. The mother has reached the "peak" of her career. From then on the grade is down.

In the meantime, her husband may have become president of the company or chairman of the board. Of course, there are not enough presidencies and chairmanships, but if the husband has been an earnest, intelligent worker, as the mother has been, he will be something fairly important—a vice-president, head of a division, production manager, head salesman, perhaps a shop boss. Of course, eventually it will be "curtains" for these men, but the curtain will come down gradually, not abruptly as it does for the wife. These men can, and usually do, continue personal and social contacts with their former fellow workers and they are welcome when they drop in at the shop or office. In the professions, the quitting whistle may never be blown excepting by death. The physician, if he has become a professor, perforce does retire, but often his services are eagerly sought by other schools. Or he is active as an emeritus. If he is a specialist, he goes on specializing. Or as a general practitioner, he gets a plaque for fifty years of practice and is urged to keep going. Old doctors never die, they just go fishing with other old doctors. Unless his brain cells atrophy, an engineer who knows his bridges or other construction, or chemistry, or electricity, need not fear. His brain power will be bid for at a high rate of prestige and money. The arts, too, smile on their devotees for a long time. The actor can make innumerable farewell appearances and when his legs give out so that he can no longer tread the boards, he can become a dramatic coach. The painter continues to paint. The sculptor to sculp; the musician to play. Or they can teach or compose. The children of their brains do not marry and depart.

Now back to the mother. The good mother finds the transition difficult; perhaps small wonder that the immature, possessive, selfish mother cannot accept it at all. You will say the inactivated mother should develop other interests and activities—club, community affairs, even politics. Yes, perhaps she should, and often she does. Yet, very understandably, many good mothers do not. After all, it is a departure, something new, rather than a continuation of their lives and chief functions, as it is with the business or professional man.

There is one man who probably understands the plight of the "retired" mother. He is the poor chap who has been "let out," possibly because of a shake-up in the organization. No longer is there a place for him. We know of several instances in which these pathetic men concealed the loss of their positions from wife and family. They would leave home each morning in time for "work," wander about aimlessly and return home after "work."

We turned aside from the Frail mother, bewailing her fate, in order to make a plea for the good, faithful mothers who have completed their jobs and are left stranded. It has been a welcome interlude. These good mothers rarely complain and they are entitled to their day in court. From all of us, and particularly from their husbands, they need more and better understanding and help. Husbands are far too prone to dismiss the situation as one of the "silly foibles" of women or, "My wife has been spoiled and she just can't take it." Or they may simply shake their heads and go and play golf.

We feel very strongly that here is a difficult and intricate problem, meriting sober reflection by both husband and wife, sympathy and mutual understanding and cooperation.

Now we may turn to the mother who is really sick and not a professional Frail.

Are you a sick mother? We mean genuinely sick, perhaps with moderate arthritis, which is painful and restricts activity? Or some impairment of the heart and circulation? Or one of dozens of other disabilities? You should not work too hard or try to do too much. Such mothers have every right to expect consideration and help from their children. If they have loved them unselfishly during childhood and looked after them, then the chances are that they will get it. But do not let your illness bind them hand and foot. Give your children their right to walk out into life and savor it.

We know dozens of mothers who carry on gallantly in spite of their physical incapacities. They have learned to accept them and live with them cheerfully. Without throwing self-preservation to the winds, yet, they encourage rather than taboo their daughters' personal and social activities. "Mother isn't well, but she doesn't complain. She's really swell. I like to have my friends in for an evening. They enjoy it." Or, says mother: "Honey, don't you dare think of not keeping your date. I feel ok and have everything I need. Skip along. Have a wonderful time. Tell me about it tomorrow." Such is the tribe of real mothers.

It is a relief to turn from the Frail mom to the "Polly-anna" mother. Usually she is a cheery little soul, bursting with kindly feelings toward all humanity. She is anxious for world peace. It is likely that she belongs to some pacifist group. And let it be recorded that many organizations are sincerely, earnestly and often intelligently, trying to halt the mass bloody orgies of war. More power to them!

The Pollyanna mother dwells with her children in the house of peace and harmony. Although her gentle soul is troubled when the boys grow very heated in their arguments with each other, yet she does recognize that males are apt to be a little on the contentious, rough side. She may interpose, "Now, Bill," "Now Paul," "Please not so loud." And that is reasonable enough.

But with the girls it is different. There may be discussions about anything, a certain kind of a dress or the personality of the biology teacher or their best girl or boy friends. The discussion waxes warm. Mother is distressed: "Alice, Joan, I'm surprised. Don't talk that way to each other. Ladies don't raise their voices. Now say you are sorry. Remember we love each other too much to quarrel." It is a beautiful ideal, a utopian sanctuary from the contest of everyday life in which women must engage as well as men.

There are a few dangers in the Pollyanna situation. Not often can the house of peace and harmony be duplicated in the outside world. There is the danger that a daughter may remain enwombed in the quiet haven. Or she may become too subdued and join the ranks of the sisterhood who have no weapons of defense and without protest take it on the chin from husbands, families, in-laws, employers. And their children are apt to get only vague and inadequate protection from them. Socially they are scarcely brilliant conversationalists. They agree almost before anyone has made an assertion. Sometimes it is their undeserved fate that their husbands become too much interested in other women who can and do maintain their own opinions. Sometimes the path of opposites is traveled and the "quiet one" becomes a social pest by the belligerency and vehemence with which she disputes every statement made, no matter how valid it might be. She is compensating for the hush-hush of her childhood.

Ladies do raise their voices. Some people think too much so. The Pollyanna mother should remember that if women had not raised their voices, and more than their voices, in the dim day of our evolutionary history, then her sex would never have obtained even the few rights and privileges which the male of the species grudgingly conceded. And her children would still be chattel to be dealt with and disposed of according to the will and whim of the father.

Today there is much about which women should and do raise their voices. There is injustice and exploitation of her sex. Her winning the right to vote is still in our memory. Properly, she has fought for the rights of her children from demanding that traffic lights be erected at dangerous corners where children were killed, to the enactment of legislation for better schools and for recreational and social opportunities and benefits. And she is for peace. That is good. In some things women are less law abiding than men. Perhaps it is a vestige from the time when they had no rights and no appeal and had to take matters into their own hands.

The Pollyanna mother should encourage differences of opinion and their expression in her daughters. She should help them to be informed so that they can present valid arguments. And she should not be too much troubled if they express them to each other emphatically. After all, emotion must enter into human relations. Except perhaps in the field of higher mathematics or pure science (even in these areas we have seen scientists tear their hair at the "stupidity" of fellow scientists) restrictedly intellectual exercises are anemic and ineffectual. Almost always the motive power of the emotions is needed. So, within reasonable limits, let your daughters argue their briefs with some determination and force. What they learn, again within limits, in the forum of childhood will serve them well in the controversial world of adults.

Then there is the "Don't You Dare Punish My Child" mother. We think of her as a mother with good intentions gone to seed. And yet she may pave the way for a hell of an adult life for her children. She has a favorite child. About half the time it is a son, the other half a daughter. Often the reasons for the channeling of her greater love and attention are unfathomable. She says she loves all her children the same. It is obvious that she does not. Unswervingly and skillfully, she tucks the favorite child behind her skirts and courageously fends off all attempts at censure from the father or the other children. The hapless victim of her protection learns all too soon that the demands made by adult life will soon negate the security the mother has provided in childhood. ˙

At times this mother comes out in the open to fight her protective war. This event can take on heroic proportions. We see the self-righteous mother giving no quarter as, bathed by the spotlight, she repulses all attacks on her and her precious child. Incidentally, her little drama will go far in inflating the child's ego and in retarding her chances of maturing.

A tacit agreement between mother and child is far more deadly than a protective battle. While the child is being punished by the father, the mother is a neutral, noninterfering bystander. But the little girl knows in advance the curtain speech of this all-too-familiar comedy. In private, mom will soothe away the hurt with rewards both material and emotional; she is proud of her "brave little girl." With infinite care mom ties the child closer and closer to herself. The nearer she draws the child, the less are the child's chances of ever being able to cut herself away.

Without being either pugnacious or devious, the true mother knows how to interpose quiet, diplomatic, intervention against unfair or oversevere criticisms of a child by the father or the other children. She does this difficult job simply and with due regard for the merits of the situation and for the personal rights of each member of the family. Her middle-of-the-road policy avoids a double hazard—the risk of dangerously inflating the child's ego or plunging it into the depths of inferiority.

The family is a mutual cooperative society. Each member has his or her responsibilities. Many mistakes will be made. Unless they are recognized and the reproof they merit is accepted, chaos will result. The girl who gets all the benefits of the cooperative and none of the blame, is unfitted to take her place in adult personal and social life. When confronted with her mistakes in school, with her companions, in her occupation and, notably, in her marriage and with her children, she will be nonplussed—perhaps sulk or weep, or become angry and hostile. Whatever the situation may be, it will deteriorate and is likely to end in dismal failure.

This brings up the question of punishment for children. Scarcely a day passes but that mothers and sometimes fathers ask us whether they should punish their children. If so, how should they be punished?

We need scarcely tell American mothers not to torture or kill their children. Cruel and unusual punishments are forbidden by the Bill of Rights. Certainly they have no place in the text of motherhood.

Of course children should be punished if they seriously misbehave. The completely permissive attitude is no longer in favor, except in a few very ultramodern "progressive" schools. Common-sense psychiatry realizes it to be inevitable that a certain amount of anxiety must and should be developed in children. Not too much. Perhaps the correct amount is that amount coming from the necessity and insistence upon conforming to minimal social standards and in respecting and adjusting to the rights of others. If no anxiety at all occurs in childhood, then when grown to adult stature, the person is misplaced, buffeted about and resentful. Unfortunately, there are many anxiety-producing situations in life. A normal amount of anxiety is protective and stimulates us to do something constructive about our problems.

Anna Freud concluded that children who were never

corrected or punished became confused and insecure. The proper kind of punishment, rightly administered, is as much a sign of loving and caring as is a caress. Children are harmed by lack of interest—not caring—and we do not mean the hypocritical business of "this is going to hurt me more than you." It is armchair stuff to say that punishment should never be given when the parent is angry. Certainly the mother will be angry at some outrageous behavior. It seems to us that long-delayed, totally non-emotional punishment is rather cold-blooded and sadistic. A child should realize why it is being punished. Usually children know, but it is safer to explain. We know adults who still do not know just what they were punished for on certain occasions in childhood or who thought they were being punished when they were not. Every mother should be rather careful that an argument with her husband, a run in her best stockings, a dispute with the grocer about his bill, or some of the other commonplaces of life, do not produce attitudes which youngsters may interpret as being disapproving of them. As we have emphasized, punishment should never be cruel. Mothers should have enough insight into the personalities of their children not to give the wrong child the wrong punishment. Some children react badly even to mild physical punishment. Various deprivations, perhaps not being permitted to go out and play, are often effective. Punishment should not produce long-lasting fear, nor should it be too deeply shaming to the child's self-respect. Almost always it should be a private matter. Finally, punishment should not be followed by long periods of coldness. Reasonably soon after the misbehavior has been understood and the punishment assimilated, the child should be re-admitted into the mother's good graces.

When a mother has a favorite child, because the child is handicapped, perhaps by the residuals of polio or some other illness, then the focusing of her interest is understandable. The handicapped child calls forth every bit of her motherly love and protection. Nevertheless, the handicapped child will have to learn to live with its handicap. Even more than the sound youngster, it will need strength and maturity to meet life on a give-and-take basis.

As readers of *Their Mothers' Sons* will remember, during World War II one of us met an Air Force hostess, who was a remarkable woman. No doubt she would object to that description. Her husband, an Air Force captain, had been killed in action. She was running a hostess house for overseas patients. She had not had any children, which was unfortunate since she was a real mother, without any "momish" nonsense about her. Her hostess house was a home, friendly and happy, but each aviator who came there was expected to try to be a grown-up man, in spite of his disabilities. He had definite responsibilities and obligations as well as privileges and fun. The men flocked to the house and brought their wives. Together with Mrs. A. they planned their futures.

Mrs. A. always wore a simple, black ribbon around her neck and her voice was just a trifle husky. I discovered that the ribbon concealed a tube inserted into the larynx, through which she breathed. There had been a very severe streptococcic throat infection in childhood with resulting stricture.

Mrs. A. talked to me about it freely. As a child she had attempted to use her difficulty in order to escape doing unpleasant things, particularly reciting lessons, which she had neglected to prepare. Her mother gently but firmly blocked the attempts at evasion and skillfully foiled her efforts to dramatize and capitalize the throat injury. One brother was very helpful. He gave "shows" to which he admitted the neighborhood children at a penny a head (two cents for the first row) to see his sister take off the ribbon and breathe through the tube. We earnestly hope that a fine young Air Force man was smart enough to see what a prize he would be getting when he married Mrs. A. We hope, too, she has many children.

The "Pretty Addlepate" is likable and amusing. Unfortunately, she may do considerable damage to her daughters. She cannot be accused of binding them too closely. On the contrary, she is often away from home, in pursuit of pleasures not even remotely maternal. Narcissus was a paragon of modesty compared to her. Her closets are full of the newest clothes; her dressing table is a mass of cosmetics, perfumes and all the other accoutrements of the lady fair. Diet and hairstyling are her religions. She is always several strides ahead of professional beauticians.

The Pretty Addlepate gets what she is after. She is pleasing to the eye, delectable to the senses. But do not misunderstand us, we do not disapprove of the artistry of feminine beauty. Like other males, we feel it has made the world a pleasanter place in which to live. We do think the Pretty Addlepate goes too far. For her little daughters, she is the acme of perfection. One little girl we know flies off into a paroxysm of weeping if there is even a vague suggestion that anyone could be as beautiful as her mother. When she kisses her children goodbye as she leaves for a party, she is a veritable fairy princess—all sweetness and beauty. As they stand in awe of this vision, they can think only of the charm and loveliness of their mother. But, unfortunately, the intoxicating aroma which cloaks her is sold in bottles; it is not the mother odor. The little girls become worshipers at the altar of beauty. They soon learn the tricks. If they marry, which is very likely, their marriages are on very shifting sands. For one thing, there is much more to marriage than feminine pulchritude. For another, no matter how skillful be the artistry applied, there comes a time when it no longer serves. Then the result is a caricature. There is no inner beauty of mind and spirit to shine forth. We knew a woman who, on her sixtieth birthday, smashed every mirror in the house and went into a profound melancholia from which she never recovered.

Little girls faithfully imitate their mothers. Sometimes their health is imperiled. Recently a group of physicians protested that the growth and vitality of young girls was being endangered, since they insisted on adhering to the strict slimming diets of their mothers. Let not the mothers of fat children preen themselves. Psychiatrists think that some mothers who stuff their children with food until they are in danger of bursting at the seams are compensating unconsciously for inner guilt at not loving or wanting their children.

It is the right and, no doubt, the duty of mothers to teach their daughters to take care of their bodies and to employ such aids to feminine beauty as are now practically standard. But the cosmetics should be mixed with common sense. Good looks and their encouragement represent only one facet of a woman's personality. There are rather more important things—intelligence, sweetness and gentleness, manners, compassion, womanliness that is more than skin deep, love of children, homemaking, and understanding of the physiology of sex and glimpses of its psychological and spiritual values. These things will outlive lipsticks and hair dyes.

Then there is the intellectual mother, as serious as the Addlepate is "flibberty-jibbity." Some Phi Beta Kappas make good mothers. Others do not. We are inclined to think that it depends somewhat on whether the educational superiority was unconsciously acquired and is chiefly used to try to demonstrate that men are inferior to women. If so, it is sadly exhibitionistic. These statements do not apply to women with superior intellectual endowments and accomplishments, who are no more exhibitionistic than men who are similarly placed. Generally they wear their honors just as modestly, which is one of the hallmarks of the true scholar.

We would like to scold the "Pseudo-Intellectual" mom. She feverishly pursues courses and goes to lectures, without ever really studying a topic or gaining a thorough knowledge of it. She trips through her garden of studies, here and there picking a flower of "knowledge." One month Shakespeare, the next political science. Modern art, French literature, nursing and geology follow in rapid succession. The Soviet crisis is hastily sandwiched somewhere in between. To her children the horn-rimmed glasses and knitted brow can be just as entrancing as the dazzlingly chic hairdo of the Pretty Addlepate. The furrowed brow often belies a mind as immature as the one under the beautiful hairdo, a mind equally ineffective in guiding the child toward a maturity based on intelligence and independence.

There is no reason in the world why even the very busy housewife should be a dumb Dora. In these days there are many sources of information—newspapers, libraries, radio, TV, neighbors. The wife and mother, for her own satisfaction and for the sake of her husband and children, should keep abreast of the times. Judging by many husbands we know, their home conversation could also stand a great deal of improvement. A divorce was granted in a Western state because the husband and wife, married for some fifteen years—now prosperous and no longer in debt—complained that they no longer had anything interesting to talk about and bored each other to extinction. The intellectual, highly educated mother can contribute very heavily to the development of her children, if she has the facility of translating her knowledge into simple, interesting terms. One such mother, a noted scholar, told her youngsters the story of the mammoth: "You children remember the big elephant you saw at the zoo last week? Well, a long time ago there were animals like him, only hairy and much bigger and fiercer. . . ." Not, "According to reports of researches upon fossils, probably imbedded during the glacial age. . . ."

We have given the main categories of more or less immature mothers, as we encounter them in our practice—the Manager, the No Trouble, the Frail, the Don't You Dare Punish My Child, the Pollyanna, the Pretty Addlepate, the Pseudo-Intellectual. There are others not so common, but who deserve mention, some of them unfavorable mention.

Among the untouchables who sully the name of "mother" are the women who, cold-bloodedly and deliberately, sell their daughters in the marriage mart to the highest bidder. It matters little whether the prospect is young or old, sound of wind and limb or decrepit, as long as he has plenty of money. In fact, the older the better, since the payoff comes sooner. There was a mother who had four daughters. She auctioned each one off to the highest bidder. The only extenuating circumstance, and it is not much, is that she was once affluent, but her circumstances were reduced and she and her daughters lived in a state of camouflaged genteel poverty. The four girls were quite beautiful of face and figure—and quite stupid. In fact, one was just a shade better than moronic. Somehow this mother borrowed and scraped together the money to send them to the best finishing schools, where they became particularly friendly with the daughters of wealthy families. The mother, adept, experienced and sophisticated, with infinite patience, taught them the social graces and how to display their good points to best advantage. The combined wealth of the four husbands amounted to much more than that many millions of dollars. Three divorces have resulted, each with a handsome settlement and, unquestionably, a generous bonus for the mother.

Not always is the mother who sells her daughters successful. One had brought the sale to the point of her young daughter's walking up the aisle on the arm of her unhappy father and in a dozen more steps she would have been joined in matrimony with the senile, but fabulously wealthy, groom-to-be. Hysteria came to her rescue. She fainted, sank to the floor, was "paralyzed" in both legs and had to be carried from the church. She recovered rapidly and in a few months married the poor, but fine young man with whom she was deeply in love. They are very happy. Our advice to the few mothers who may be tempted is brief: "Don't do it."

There are mother-daughter transactions which, though they do not involve offering young female flesh on the auction block, nevertheless are dubious. True enough, usually the mothers are activated by a desire to help their daughters, but . . .

Recently there was quite an uproar in Rimini, Italy. The judges were selecting Miss Italy. The police ordered fourteen lovely young girls barred, because they were under eighteen. A government directive rules that no minor may parade before judges in the Miss Italy contest.

Furious mothers assembled in front of the judges' quarters and warned they were going to sue the government for "loss of time, money and dignity."

We think also of those misguided mothers who abandon bed and board, go to Hollywood, deplete the family finances, suffer personal privations and haunt the casting offices in the hope of making movie stars of their little daughters. Poor children! Almost never do they succeed. And, when very rarely they do, then the chances of success combined with happiness are almost nil. The mother has about the same odds of realizing her ambitions as she would have in making a fortune by feeding coins into a one-arm bandit.

Probably we are old-fashioned, but we do not enjoy seeing little girls displaying their permanents on TV for a fee. They seem too young to have permanents and the exhibition is not good for their egos. We could also get on very well without quiz-kid programs.

There is a vivacious mother, not openly narcissistic about her physical charms, yet self-loving and exhibitionistic in her personality. She craves attention. No matter what may be the occasion, even though she starts as a spectator in the last row of the balcony, she ends up in the center of the stage. She is not above competing with her daughters for the attentions of their beaux. She would be genuinely shocked to realize this, even though sometimes it is common neighborhood gossip: "Mary Jane better look out or her mother will cut her out with her boy friend." Mother is on hand to welcome and entertain Jack while Mary Jane is dressing for her date. She cavorts and prances and talks incessantly in sophisticated fashion. Jacks vary in their reactions. Some of them are quite fascinated by what they interpret as the personal interest of "a woman of the world." Others may begin to wonder about Mary Jane. Her mother is "kind of strange." Mary Jane herself is apt to be embarrassed and torn by conflicting loyalties. Children may be a bit "wild" themselves, but they are usually conservative about their mothers. Mary Jane may try to explain her mother to Jack. She does it badly and her budding romance may wither and die.

Mothers should meet their daughters' beaux and get to know them. And they need not be stiff and stuffy with them. They can be pleasant, interested and likable, without sacrificing that quiet, womanly dignity which goes with being a mother and which a young man hopes to find in his girl's mother.

The exhibitionistic mother does not know how to grow

old gracefully. It is not necessarily a painful process. From each decade of life the best things can be carried forward into the next decade, suitably modified. At the same time, there is a receptive attitude and enthusiasm to the new possibilities that are offered. A girl of seventeen or eighteen would not want to play with dolls as she did when she was five. Probably she is thinking of having babies. Possibly she has already had one and will be having more in the next two decades of her life. At fifty or sixty, it is unlikely that she will have babies, but it is likely that there will be grandchildren. In them she will find a renaissance of her motherhood. So in this way, in the matter of giving life, in her love and marriage, in homemaking, in occupations, intellectual and recreational pursuits, life has continuity and purpose, instead of merely being a series of isolated events.

All normal mothers are anxious for their daughters to marry. It does not mean that they want to be rid of them. Some mothers are too eager and too alert to get their daughters wedded. Perhaps they have been frightened by statistics which show more females at the marriageable age than men. In any event, such mothers coach their daughters just how to act, how to talk and, indeed, how to think with every prospective suitor. Betty or Alice dreads coming home from a date because mom's eyes will be two interrogation marks and there will come the question, direct or implied, "Did he?" This attitude is likely to make the girl jittery and she does not acquit herself too well with the young man she hopes to marry. She is distracted, thinking about just what she is going to say to her mother when she gets home.

No doubt our readers have met, as we have, mothers who were disappointed in the sex of the new arrival. Usually they do not voice their disappointments, but from their expressions, attitudes and manner, it is obvious. A few may even say, "Oh, it's a boy. I wanted a girl." Or, "Goodness, another girl." Fathers are traditionally expected to want a son and they subscribe to tradition consciously. Unconsciously there is more reason why the father should want a daughter. Nevertheless, if it is a daughter, he passes out the cigars with an apologetic air.

Usually none of these attitudes are too serious or do any harm. In the vast majority of cases they are soon dispelled by the happiness of having a baby. Occasionally they remain and then they are harmful. There are a few instances in which mothers continue to protest their frustration. We know of one woman who would not allow her little boy to play with toys suitable for a boy and instead gave him dolls. She dressed him as a girl until he was ten years old and then desisted only because of outraged neighborhood opinion. We have known mothers who in lesser degree manifested disapproval of the sex of a child. If her little daughter misbehaved, such a mother might say, "I wish you were a boy. I wanted a boy. Girls are so much trouble." Or if there is a son, she might give him much more affectionate interest. These things are serious and dangerous. The little girl feels misplaced, not wanted. It is possible that into her budding personality there will be engrafted the beginnings of pathological feminism or even lesbianism.

We are about to close this chapter. Some of our readers might exclaim, "Why, they forgot about sex. Don't they know that the mother who gives her daughters a distorted picture of sex and who may describe it to them as something unpleasant and even loathsome, an unfair burden placed upon women, is the most dangerous of all moms?" No, we have not forgotten. We know it all too well. We have reserved a separate chapter for this mom. Many of the immature mothers we have described are likable and some are admirable. The mother who defrauds her children, particularly her daughters, by implanting wrong and pathological ideas about sex into their personalities, is neither admirable or likable. She is detestable.

Chapter VIII

SEX

WE DO not intend to open wide the door of the cabinet of horrors containing the records of sexual crimes perpetrated upon children. Our readers know there are such depths of human depravity. They are of interest chiefly to psychiatrists, sociologists and the law. Sometimes children are subjected by their parents to various sexual perversions. There is recorded an instance in which a couple cruelly whipped their little daughter in order to stimulate themselves sexually. There is incest, more common than is generally realized. It must be remembered that it is a throwback, an anachronism. Probably at one time in our troubled phylogenetic history, it was not as strictly taboo as it is in our culture. Incest more often involves father and daughter, but it may occur between mother and son. It is the motif of the great tragedy *Oedipus Rex*. We have encountered "near" incest between mother and son a number of times. In everything but actual physical sexual relations, it is incest—the mother making love to her son, fondling and kissing him, sleeping with him. At a social gathering we saw such a mother stage a jealous tantrum because her nineteen-year-old son danced with one of the young girls. And there is psychological incest not overtly exhibited, but apparent to the skilled psychiatrist from the facial expression, the voice inflection and the gestures of the mother, showing that unconsciously the mother is thinking of her son as her lover.

We are more concerned now in telling how mothers, by grievous errors of omission and commission, may distort the future sex life of their daughters and cause untold misery. Our gambit is the presentation of a few case notes selected only because they represent frequently occurring situations; because they cover a fairly wide range and because they have the common backgrounds of the failure of mothers to give their daughters a reasonably fair perspective about sex. In these patients there was almost a complete lack of information in preparing the daughters for the sexual function or it consisted of gloomy forebodings and warnings about the sexual tyranny of the male and his enslavement of the female and/or the physical and mental misery caused by sex.

A married woman of thirty certainly had her attention fixed on her genitourinary region. At one interview she told us that this part of the body was never referred to by her mother, even remotely. She herself did not like to refer to it. Mrs. M. complained that she was always "running to the bathroom," that she had pain "there"—vaguely indicating the sex organs—fatigue, headache, nausea, vertigo, backache. All these symptoms were much intensified whenever "he wants me." Then she becomes frantic with anxiety. "I am afraid I will be permanently injured." She confessed readily enough that she had never had an orgasm, never had enjoyed sexual relations, and now "hated it." Her best performance was when she succeeded in making herself indifferent and traced in her mind the pattern of the wallpaper in the bedroom. Apparently there are many women who have never had an orgasm, or at most, a very fragmentary one. Of course, there are many explanations. A few instances are physically determined. More are largely the fault of the husband. However, the overwhelming majority are psychologically conditioned and certainly a significant factor is the inculcation into the personality of faulty sex attitudes during childhood.

We treated a middle-aged woman who was repeating two failures of her own mother in her distaste and abhorrence of sexual relations and in mistakenly suspecting her husband of infidelity. In her mother's case the situation had terminated in divorce. Our patient was sound enough physically, but worried about her heart. Finally, late one night when her husband returned from a meeting, she had a "heart attack"—gasping for breath, tossing about, clutching wildly at her chest. The frightened husband sent for the family doctor, who said the heart seemed all right and it was probably indigestion. However, the attacks continued, one almost every night the husband had to go out. He had to tell her just where he could be reached. A cardiologist reported a completely normal heart. With psychiatric help the patient came to realize that the "heart attacks" were an unconscious defense against, and rationalization of, the unwillingness to accept sexual life, coupled with the unjustified suspicion that her husband was "carrying on" with another woman. With her understanding there came shame and tears. There were a few more slight attacks and then they ceased. The patient is now better adjusted and happier.

A girl not yet in her twenties, whose childhood was rigidly puritanical, sex particularly being taboo, already has had more sex life than the average woman in her lifetime. There have been at least forty men in her sexual life. Not that she has ever found sexual satisfaction. She rushes frantically from one affair to another and fills in the interim with lurid sexual fantasies. She is a nymphomaniac. Nymphomania is really frigidity in which for one reason or another, sexual satisfaction cannot be achieved. This unfortunate young woman illustrates the futility of attempting to fulfill a function by splitting off one part of it. Torn out of its matrix of love and the many things that go with it, the physical sex act alone becomes a caricature and a mockery.

Another girl in her late teens is slowly overcoming the effect of sex bans which her unhappily married mother laid down in her childhood. Several times Margaret has attempted suicide. Often when she was growing up, her mother told her that if she ever brought a boy into the house, she would horsewhip her. This did not set Margaret against marriage, but had the roundabout result that for a long time she felt that if she married and had a male child, she would murder him.

For several years Mrs. X., an intelligent woman forty years old, was in the grip of a torturing obsessive-compulsive neurosis. Her obsessions were focussed upon dirt, contamination, infection. She would pick up the menstrual cloths with tweezers, burn them and then bury the ashes and the tweezers. She scrubbed the genitosexual parts of

her body many times a day and applied antiseptics until
they were irritated and inflamed. Often expensive under-
wear and dresses were burned because she felt they might
have become contaminated. She retained her sense of
humor and remarked that she was under the shower more
than elsewhere and that the soap and water bill was terrific.
She was devoted to her husband, but he himself realized
even after many years of marriage, that to hint at sexual
relations would precipitate a panic. No, Mrs. X. was not
insane. With her intellectual mind she realized how silly
and irrational was her behavior, but she was powerless to
control it. She remembered clearly that during her childhood her mother regarded sex gloomily and referred to it
as unclean and sinful. Her mother was a deeply religious
woman and fulfilled the sexual obligation of her marriage
no doubt with shame and guilt. At best, she felt that
marriage gave a certain amount of moral and legal sanction
to a horrible practice.

Schizophrenia is the most prevalent psychosis, which each
year snatches thousands of young people from the world
of the mentally alive and retires them to mental hospitals,
often to remain permanently, to dream away their lives.
There never was a case of schizophrenia in which the sex
pattern was not prominent in its clinical warp and woof.
Usually it can be traced back to childhood. The fantasies
of patient after patient are filled with sexual preoccupations,
ruminations, weird delusions. Rarely in the psychoses are
the physical facts of sexual relations faced or even implied.
Schizophrenic girls and women are forever having babies,
but by non-carnal conception, as for instance by being forced
to bathe in a tub in which a man had bathed previously.

Nothing in a psychosis can appear suddenly from the clear blue sky. It is reasonable to assume that these distorted and fantastic misconceptions had their roots in childhood and certainly sometimes in the defective soil of a mother-child relationship. When adult life demands an acceptance of the realism of heterosexual life, the fragile, often markedly introverted personality shrinks from the issue. Of course, these things are not the cause of schizophrenia. It would be an oversimplification of a very complicated illness. But they are factors which stand out too prominently to be disregarded. The schizophrenic is afraid of life, and sex is the pulse of life.

We had not intended to present a clinic of patients, but perhaps it is just as well. The patients do show the delayed and dangerous effects of disregard of a child's sexual development. However, we are more concerned about the human beings who do not go to psychiatrists. And we particularly focus our attention upon the daughters of mothers who have been sexual traitors to them and to their own sex. So often, and so sadly, these daughters have been broken upon the wheel of sex and condemned to drag out frustrated and miserable lives. This is not to say that the mother who gives her daughters sound perspectives about sex, as many mothers do, can be assured that all will be well in their future lives. They have given them considerable insurance, but it does not always pay off. There may be destructive factors beyond the mother's control, in the circumstances of life or perhaps in the personality of the girl. Nevertheless, sex insurance taken out in childhood is worth many times the premium.

Too much ado about sex? We think not. There seems

to be a general idea that psychiatrists think and talk of nothing else, that they literally wallow in sex. True enough, in their professional lives they do give a great deal of attention to sex. If they did not, they would scarcely be fit to be students of human behavior. To the square clinical inch, in the psychoses, in the neuroses, and more importantly in human predicaments, frustrations and un-happiness, there are more ingredients derived from sex problems than from anything else. Day after day, patient after patient unrolls before us the long list of conflicts and inhibitions which impede or prevent the fulfillment of the natural sexual function. Contrariwise, in men and women who are sexually well adjusted, either in fact or in their understanding, there seems to be less tension and an easier accomplishment of other life objectives.

Of course, merely the ability to perform the sexual act is not synonymous with satisfactory sexual adjustment. Or in itself is it helpful. Far from it.

Comparison of man with other animals does not help much. One of our lay friends said to us, "Why all this dither about sex? Look at pigs. They have plenty of sex and no trouble." Incidentally, we made a few inquiries and found that occasionally pigs do have trouble. More pertinent is the fact that the sex life of pigs and other animals is strictly biological. In our species, which has an infinitely more complicated cerebral structure than that of animals, the sex act is, or should be, set in a matrix of love, tenderness, protection, etc.

Nature made sex very important and demanding in order to insure the procreative drive and our multiplication and survival. In primitive days, with the threat of prehistoric animals, unchecked disease, wars and famine taking a large toll of life, survival was difficult. Our civilized life, culture and mores, as we subscribe to them, tend to block the free expression of sex and aggression, more than any other instincts. Much of this is necessary. Otherwise the social and legal codes would be flagrantly flouted and there would be chaos. Accordingly, more than any other function, sex has been heavily veneered and distorted by many successive cultures. Yet it retains its primitive aspects and will continue to retain them. In one sense the irresistible force (sex) meets the immovable object (civilization).

Mothers and fathers may resort to easy, but rather dubious, ways of keeping the virtue of daughters intact. Virtue is an excellent thing; some thought should be given as to just how it is insured. One method, a good method, is for mothers to inculcate into the personalities of young girls by precept, but much more by example, discernment and judgment, the realism of sex, but also a sense of its fineness and fitness, and its ideals. This is tedious, but by far the best plan. An easier and sometimes effective method of obtaining virtue is by harsh judgments, punishments, condemnation and the production of overwhelming guilt. We do not believe the end justifies the means, here or elsewhere. The result in the daughter, even if she remains virtuous, which is dubious, is apt to be sexually disastrous— limited vision, rigid and condemnatory attitudes, partial or even complete frigidity.

Prudishness is neither virtuous nor moral. Or at best, it is morality gone to seed. Of course, "naturalness" can go too far. While we cannot vouch for it, we were told of a little girl in whose home clothes were regarded as something to wear outside the house, and bathroom doors were never closed. The first time she visited a little girl friend, she was embarrassed because the adults wore clothes and closed the door when they were in the bathroom.

In spite of their seemingly casual attitudes, and often reckless behavior, boys and girls are very vulnerable to deep and strong guilt feelings. A system of rewards, warnings, threats and lurid accounts of sexual sins, resulting in punishments, from ostracism to death, followed by damnation and hell, can hardly help filling a child with a blind, unreasoning sense of guilt, so deeply imbedded that he or she cannot eradicate it in a lifetime. It is remarkable that we so readily forget we were once children. If we remembered, we would know how great and heroic and *infallible* were the mother and father figures. As children we were weak and insecure and could not reason. We needed parental approval for our emotional sustenance and confidence. Otherwise, we would have perished emotionally. Obviously, youngsters identify with parents, particularly girls with their mothers. They imitate and emulate in everything—looks, opinions, attitudes, behavior, social and moral customs.

By the time the child, and particularly the daughter, is old enough to think for herself, mother's thinking and habits have become so deeply ingrained that they cannot be wholly erased. Not even if the behavior of the children is in direct opposition to them. They are still there, deep down in us and they will be expressed directly or deviously. Sometimes as adults, after doing some inconsequential act, in itself certainly blameless, we experience an uneasy feeling tinged with guilt. Our pleasure is spoiled and our judgment impaired. Somewhere in the hidden cloisters of the psyche, a small bell has sounded: "Mother would not approve." Usually the guilt is buried deeply in the unconscious. The marriage of a beautiful and intelligent girl to a fine young man was strained to the breaking point, because of her complete inability to tolerate sexual relations. She was "frigid." Consciously she felt that relations between husband and wife not only were right, but desirable. She felt that something must be wrong with her physically. Only a long and painful course of treatment opened the recesses of her mind and revealed to her that when she was a child her mother's remarks about the "nastiness of sex" and "the vileness and selfishness of men" still gripped her innermost, hidden being. Even though it was right "outside," "inside" it was still wrong and, therefore, there could be no pleasure in it. When this was worked through, the "frigidity" disappeared completely.

Even little girls cannot and should not be constantly at home with mother. They should sally forth into the great unknown spaces of "outside." They make contacts with things outside the home and the growth principle is stimulated. Of course, the perimeter of their activities is quite limited. Very importantly they run little errands for mother to the corner store. Or pay a surprise visit to a playmate just around the corner. Perhaps, in the suburbs, to a vacant lot to gather a bunch of flowers for mother. Sometimes they just wander away for a short distance, enjoying the excitement of being independent. As they grow older, the range of activity lengthens and becomes more purposeful. School athletics, visits to friends after school, to the corner drugstore, parties, a bus trip to a neighboring city to see in person a "divine" crooner, school dances, teen dates. Not always do they notify mother in advance where they are going, and they may be a bit vague as to where they have been. For some reason a little secrecy puts a sheen of glamour on the most casual engagement. Then, too, many young girls are at the peak of the daydreaming age. It is so much easier to daydream while walking along a quiet street or lonely road, than it is at home where her brother Tom makes so much noise or teases her for being "dopey." And who knows, perhaps the knight in shining armor, or in these days the captain of the school football team, may suddenly appear and declare his undying love.

All these things are wholesome and good. There is a little peril. Occasionally a terrible thing happens, which fills the hearts of the parents with horror and sadness, and sometimes the community and the nation. A little girl may be kidnapped. A girl may be cornered by a pervert and made to view his indecent exposure. Some perversion may be forced upon her. She may be raped, sometimes also tortured and murdered. All these things have happened and will happen again. Naturally, the public press reports them with scare headlines. The crime is burned into the minds of all decent citizens. So we forget that, blessedly, these occurrences are rare. True enough, statistics are no comfort to the heartbroken parents. Yet, what can be done beyond sensible precautions and good police protection and severe laws? Certainly not every girl can be constantly attended, never permitted to go out alone. Think of the retarding effect and damage to the personalities of hundreds of thousands of youngsters. While there should be suffi-cient publicity, neighborhood hysteria and wild excitement only make the situation rather worse for the victim and frighten the other children. Too, it may produce an unhealthy curiosity, morbid conversation and rumination among the children.

Should a little girl suffer a psychological sexual wound, it is a supreme test of a mother, not only of her capacity to handle the crisis, but of her whole record as a mother. In all likelihood the child will run home in a panic, screaming with terror. The mother will hold her closely, cover her with kisses, softly murmuring endearing sounds. Then the mother goes into her role of the Master Psychotherapist. Though her inner anxiety is great, she does not let too much of it show. Alarm is contagious. She gets the facts, but does not hurry the recital. She does not stay the flood of tears or other evidences of emotion. She reassures, but does not make too light of what happened. She does not try to wipe it out of memory: "Don't ever think of it again." In other words, the mother establishes close identification and transference with her daughter. She is interested and takes a careful history without hurrying the child. She does not block emotional outpouring, since, intuitively, she knows it is an important part of the healing process. She does not encourage repression, since she senses that emotionally highly charged material simply pushed under the top layer of consciousness will crop up later on and cause trouble. She has a few more talks with her daughter to combat introspection. Even the greatest psychiatrist could do no more than this mother does and perhaps not as much.

We extract two case records from our files, which have certain similarities and certain differences. Two little girls were about the same age. They sustained about the same psychic shock; each one cornered by a pervert, who exposed himself and made the child touch his sexual organs. Betty had the kind of a mother we have described. The psychic wound was healed. The memory of it gradually blurred, though it was not completely erased. There was a scar, but it was a very small scar.

Anne's mother was capable and just and a little on the stern side. She loved her children, but was not given to demonstrations of affection. She insisted upon obedience and Anne *had* gone out for a walk when she was told to stay at home. So Anne was too afraid and ashamed to tell her mother. For a long time she battled with her shame and guilt and then, when her ego could no longer tolerate it, she repressed it. From then on her life was beclouded. She married and had two children. But her marriage was below par. She felt uneasy with men and could never quite trust them. Her sexual adjustment was very faulty. At the age of forty, thirty-one years after her childhood sexual shock, she developed a psychoneurosis. After a long and arduous period of treatment, which brought the early repressed material into the searchlight of consciousness, she finally made a reasonably good adjustment.

We have not quite finished. We have a few more remarks to make about the most dangerous of all moms, the one who tries to destroy her daughter's future sexual happiness. This mother performs an emotional abortion upon her own child. We could almost wish that such an operation would be declared criminal and made punishable by law. This biologically unnatural mother, MOM, mercilessly strips sex of all its beauty and turns it into an abhor-

rent and disgusting thing. Unconsciously she is wreaking
her vengeance on her children for the inadequacies and
failures of her own sexual life. She can accomplish this
end directly or indirectly, as she reveals the "facts of life"
to her daughters. She leaves the impression on a daughter
of tender age—sending out tentative shoots into womanhood—that men are little more than lustful birds of prey,
waiting to swoop down and carry off unsuspecting
females. "A woman can't be too careful. Men are hardly
ever considerate when it comes to 'that.' They don't care
what a woman has to go through or how much her health
suffers, as long as they satisfy themselves."

The real mother imparts to her children a sound and
healthy perspective on sex. She does not feel the need to
sing a hymn to Venus or a dirge of sexual hate. Her own
failures and frustrations are kept out of the picture. She
has accepted and profited by her mistakes. They are not
inflicted on her children. Conversely, sex is not painted
all in rosy hues, with no allowance made for responsibility
and the importance for keeping a steady balance between
give and take. Sane attitudes emerge from the mother's
general reaction when the topic of sex comes up casually;
very little is to be gained by planned and formal instruction.
She avoids starry-eyed platitudes and soothing clichés. She
does not go into every detail or make a blueprint, for she
knows that the stifling of spontaneity can be calamitous,
and that the fashioning of one's sex life after that of another is doomed to failure. Sex is not divested of all its
trappings; enough of its inner veilings are left untouched,
so that the child will not be deprived of the maturing values
and satisfactions of making her own discoveries in later

life. The mother desires only to give her daughters straight-forward information in the hope of producing a basic core of receptive and favorable ideas in the matter of sex. She can then wish them well as they begin their sexual journeys through life, firm in the knowledge that they will at least have a chance not to fall too often or seriously and that they are well on their way to attaining a mature sexual happiness.

What about those mothers who tell their daughters nothing at all about sex, leaving them to pick up information wherever they can? Amazingly, there are many mothers in this group. Not usually are these women neglectful because they "don't care." More often it is because they are shy, hesitant, even prudish about talking these things over with their daughters. Unconsciously they are staking out large areas of future maladjustment and unhappiness for their daughters. From lack of knowledge and wrong information about sex there is a large and withered harvest —illicit relations, illegitimate pregnancies, sometimes followed by criminal abortions and death, suicides, promiscuity, prostitution, seduction, rape, venereal disease, abnormal sex behavior.

Fairly often we have witnessed startling and serious consequences following the failure to impart authentic information in preparation for the first menstrual period. There may be great anxiety with frightened preoccupation about having been injured internally, or having sinned, or being punished. One girl at her first period, for which she had not been prepared at all, had an acute mental attack during which she had vivid and terrifying hallucinations of being "stabbed by a terrible man with a livid scar across his cheek."

Gladys Denny Shultz in her book, *It's Time You Knew* (J. B. Lippincott Company, Philadelphia, 1955), gives some excellent advice based on the plea of a fine seventeen-year-old girl who said, "Girls came to our prep school at fourteen or fifteen, and felt out of the dormitory discussions because there were so many words they didn't know. They didn't like to show their ignorance by asking—it made them feel so young and inexperienced. So they would go right on feeling young and inexperienced and inferior to the girls who know these things. Also, it seemed to me that the discussions were valuable in helping us get our ideas sorted out. The girls who didn't know what was being talked about could hardly get the full value from them."

Among the "so many words they didn't know" were these: Abortion, adultery, age of consent, bastard, fornication, gestation, gynecologist, illegitimacy, illicit relations, miscarriage, mistress, pornography, promiscuity, prostitute, rape, seduction, sublimation, venereal disease, exhibitionism, homosexuality, frigidity, nymphomania, "Peeping Toms."

The good, mature mother will not constitute herself a forum lecturer to her daughters on the meaning of these words and other sex information. But she will be ready to impart information to her daughters when the opportunity arises and occasionally she will make the opportunity. As she gives information she should not be too puritanically rigid and prudish and certainly she should not be the figure of the threatening and avenging angel of righteousness. A good test is her capacity to distinguish between "necking," which is friendly and not unwholesome, and "petting," which is dangerously apt to lead to illicit relationships.

We feel we have left something unsaid. There is an ennobling spiritual quality in sex which cannot be confined in a frame of words. Men and women, the best of them, have made of sex something beautiful. Perhaps these are still in the minority, but it is an insistent minority, which determines the upward swing of evolution. Considering that the superego (conscience) is a few paltry thousand years old and still a puny thing, we may be astonished that they have taken stark sex, a dominant part of our most ancient heritage, the id, and clothed it with love and beauty, sacrifice, the desire to give and not only to take. A soul has been breathed into an ape.

Chapter IX

FEMINISM—THE BIOLOGICAL REJECTION

UNFORTUNATELY, "feminism" and "femininity" sound too much alike. By femininity we understand the biological motivation and psychological art of being a woman. We interpret feminism as the deep wish to compete with men, not because it may be necessary or the circumstances of life demand it, but prompted by the desire to prove the male is inferior to the female. It expresses dissatisfaction with being a woman and some degree of hostility toward men.

In order to appreciate the course of events and the psychological ingredients which may go into the making of a feminist, it is useful to give a preview of the comparative situations confronting the male and the female child. As she grows, the little girl soon follows a somewhat different psychological path in life from that of the little boy. For both boy and girl, the first and greatest love is the mother. Soon, however, the paths of their loves diverge. In some ways the little boy has a less complicated problem. Unless it is blocked by his mother's unwillingness or inability to receive it, his love for his mother is simple and direct. Of course, he loves his father too, but in a different way. His love is tinged with envy for what he considers to be the prior claim of his father on his mother. Envy, but admiration, too, for the superior strength, knowledge and ability of his father. In his love there is the strong desire to be like his father. The father serves as the model into which the little boy would like to make himself. His mother love is filled with tenderness befitting a mother, the all-giving person, who by her care and protection provides the psychological soil which permits him to survive and grow. He likes to imagine that one day he will be as big and strong as his father and then he will be able to love mother as father does and have her all to himself. At the same time his sense of reality warns him of the unlikelihood of his dream's ever coming true. In his childish mind, too, he fears that his father, if he knew of his little fantasies and plans concerning mother, would disapprove and, perhaps, retaliate. From this, it is easy to see that the little boy's love for his mother is comparatively without admixture, while his love for his father is strongly tinged with feelings of rivalry, resentment, fear. This classical situation has been more or less understood and appreciated by men since very early times. We have noted that the great Greek tragedy, *Oedipus Rex*, portrays in allegory the incest motif. Modern psychoanalysts refer to this father-son-mother situation as the "Oedipus conflict."

All this is simple enough compared with the mixed reactions experienced by the little girl. In infancy and as a small child, the constant care by the mother and their close and intimate contact make the mother the outstandingly important adult in her love life. The opportunities for contacts with father are, of course, much less. As time goes on, however, the girl-child becomes aware of the difference in sexes and she feels the same kind of erotically tinged love for her father that her brother feels toward his mother. Shocking? Certainly not. It is all a perfectly natural part of children's development and, if successfully completed, the love of children for their parents of the opposite sex is the basis for a healthy and happy marriage in later life. Psychologically speaking, each boy marries his mother and each girl her father. To be sure, this is scarcely observable in a mature marriage, but in an immature or pathological marriage the parent-child relationship is often seen and commented on by friends and relatives.

As she grows up, the little girl has, to some extent, to make a shift in her feelings. She is biologically drawn to men by virtue of the ancient plans of nature. Now, the father becomes the person to whom her strongest feelings are attached. Her original mother love becomes tinctured more or less strongly with submerged feelings of envy and hostility, analagous to those the boy feels for his father and for the same reasons. It is the typical feeling of the "have-nots" for the "haves," readily observable in personal, political and social life. The little girl's beautiful and fanciful daydreaming romances with father as the hero are doomed by reality. She is forced to face the fact that her mother has the prior claim. In the usual normal, healthy, family life the girl is able to accept and reconcile herself to the obvious and inevitable situation. She decides that she will have to wait until she is grown up. Then, though she cannot get "Daddy," she can get in his place another man like him who will be able to fulfill all her wishes. Then her daydreaming and her thinking become more direct and purposeful and there emerges the concept of love for the opposite sex. We repeat that in the successful solution of these child-loves there is laid the foundation for happy and successful adult marriages.

Nevertheless, in the process of growing up the little girl does make a shift from her first love choice (the mother) to a second (the father). It is an extra step, an added hurdle to be negotiated and therefore it raises the possibility of difficulties. These obstacles may occasionally force the girl into the path of feminism. This extra step and its accompanying difficulties and risks may account for the fact that there are more neuroses among women than men. The penalty sometimes paid may range from simple maladjustment or minor disturbances of character, to "nervous breakdowns" or even psychoses. Incidental factors help shape the final outcome—the magnitude of the unsolved problem, the degree to which common sense and reliance have been developed in the girl, native intelligence and a sound, healthy body.

There is still another hazard for the small girl, particularly if she has brothers or, as she often does, plays with boys. It is the bogy of physical strength and prowess. Children give physical strength a much higher rating than do adults. Therefore, little girls often are bitterly envious of their brothers and male playmates who are stronger, can run faster, walk on their hands, turn handsprings, etc. Little boys, being little boys, rarely miss the opportunity to bring this gloatingly to the attention of the little girls, and they are relegated to the ranks of the "sissie-pants"

along with the boys who fall short of the physical criteria
of the cult of boyhood.

Under favorable conditions when the little girl feels herself valued and regarded as reasonably important because
of her feminine traits and/or the rivalry with her mother
and the boys is not too pressing, there may not be any
difficulty. Unfortunately, however, and frequently, such
ideal conditions do not obtain and the girl develops feelings of insufficiency and inadequacy because she is a girl.
She may come to envy boys deeply and her most pleasing
daydreams are, that in spite of everything, one day she
will be magically transformed into a boy.

Several situations tend to bring the boy vs. girl conflict
into pathological areas. One is that the girl feels that her
brothers are more wanted and favored. In another a strong
mother dominates the family and a weak father is a passive
bystander. The girl feels her love is spurned. She feels
rejected and insignificant. She is being unjustly discriminated against by her mother and brothers. And she cannot even count on her father to take her part.

Such a conflict may also arise when the father takes
little interest in the family and is seldom home. The death
of the father entails the same risk. Interesting and well
worth noting, is the fact that small children are seldom able
to grasp the true meaning of death and are apt to view it as
desertion or abandonment on the part of the deceased parent. The little girl thinks and sometimes even says, "Daddy
can do anything he wants to do. He wouldn't have gone
away and left me if he really cared anything about me."

In the situations we have outlined it is not hard to understand that the small girl may not be completely victorious

in the inner childish struggle of conflicting loves, fears, resentments, envies and belittlements. She may succeed in making a compromise and in coming to some sort of terms with the demands of adult life without a breakdown. But, often, the adjustment is faulty and her capacity to live happily and completely is seriously impaired. Life for her becomes a maze from which she should have been given the opportunity to find her way out during childhood.

1. She may be able for the time to bring her rebellious feelings into line and make a fairly successful marriage. But, sometimes, years later she may fail to overcome the obstacles so common in all human relationships or imposed by the practical demands of the world in which we live. Then she may regress or retreat psychologically. This is in line with a general principle of human behavior, when one is confronted with a painful, anxiety-producing and apparently unsolvable situation. Then there is in the attempt to get peace of mind, the temptation to go backward, to step down on the ladder of maturity. For the girl this would be the rung of her original mother relationship. If this relationship was a satisfactory and happy one, then the retreat may bring the desired peace of mind. If, however, it was frustrating and unhappy then the retreat serves only to bring the unhappy past to life in the present. In other words, she then, and without consciously realizing it, repeats with her husband over and over again, all the childhood conflicts with her mother. Once again, she is the confused and wretched child seeking to force, with the weapons of childhood, the mother love she once was denied.

2. She may renounce both femininity and sex. This type of woman is apt to remain single. Though she may be able to form somewhat distant, intellectual, overidealized relationships with men, yet her real feelings and energies will be devoted to a career. We scarcely need to state here that such sublimation can be successful. The lives of very many fine women are ample proof of this. Some of these women seem to come through without psychological scars or at least scars so small that they are negligible. However, many do not come through emotionally. Their drive in life is based on a denial of strong and deep-rooted instincts which are constantly knocking at the door of consciousness demanding expression. It is not at all surprising that such attempted sublimations frequently fail.

3. She may or may not marry but, in either case, the prominent pattern in the warp and woof of her life will be woven from the threads of rebuffed childhood love, engendering envy, resentment, bitterness, hostility. Behind the portals of the conscious mind, these stirrings motivate and guide her behavior and largely determine her thinking. Deep down she never forgets that once she yearned to be a boy. There is the ferment of her inner feelings toward boys because of their assumed superiority and her disappointment and disillusionment that her sex could not be changed. Her wishes and fantasies were not realized. Never did she become a boy.

An intelligent woman who came to us as a pronounced feminist, has made much progress. Her dress, her manner and attitude toward males have become gratifyingly feminine. She is almost a woman. Yet she still clings to her childhood fantasies of becoming a boy. "You have accomplished a great deal for me and I am happier, but you will never get me to give up an occasional daydream about being a man."

In some of these groups, notably in the third, there are numbered some of the women who make life hell on earth for their husbands. The angry wife has rejected her womanliness but she cannot turn off the menstrual flow nor can she always withhold sexual intercourse, pregnancy and childbearing. Many husbands try to be helpful. True enough it is often in clumsy ineffectual fashion, but they do try. Nevertheless, they do not escape the stinging whiplash of their wives' tongues. The "suffering" and contempt may be silently and sullenly expressed by attitude and manner. Often it erupts into words: "If you had the curse, you wouldn't be so blithe and gay. I just wish you could have it once and suffer as I do." Or, "Look at me, all bloated and out of shape with a baby on the way and God only knows what I will suffer. I wish you had to have a baby just once. Then you would know. I suppose you are very pleased with what you did to me." Or, "Men get all the breaks. We women just suffer." It is as if somewhere in the deep, dark recesses of the psyche, these women invoke the law of the talon: "You are a man. I wish I were a man. I hate you because you represent what I wanted to be. In revenge I will do all I can to make you suffer."

Of course children, particularly girls, growing up in this kind of atmosphere, learn by heart the litany of "What women have to suffer." Naturally the daughters' preview of sex and marriage becomes considerably biased.

A masterly short story by Conan Doyle tells of a district doctor called to deliver a baby in the slums of London.

The husband was seated beside his wife, one hand under the sheet. The doctor thought he was holding his wife's hand, to comfort her in her labor. Suddenly the husband fainted. The doctor stripped back the bed sheet and to his horror found that the wife had put a chain around her husband's wrist. With each labor pain she twisted the free end of the chain. It had cut through almost to the bone. It was her revenge for an unwanted pregnancy and labor.

Parents, particularly mothers, often say to a small child, "I'm going to eat you up." The child chuckles with pleasure over the joke and pretends to be terrified. But many a truth is spoken in jest and some of the women we have described, as little girls were almost literally devoured by their mothers. Their thoughts and feelings, their minds, were almost completely taken over—psychologically ingested.

By the same token and because sometimes this is the only kind of love these children knew, they mistake it for real love and assimilate all its patterns and artifices. Often, as adult women, the only relationship they are able to have with their own husbands and children is possessive, dominating, devouring.

Freud, and later Abraham, presented a hypothetical but interesting interpretation of the ancient and widespread spider phobia: according to them the spider represents the angry mother of whom the child is afraid. It is the wicked mother who ensnares and devours her helpless little children. We had some verification of the hypothesis in the study of the material of an analysis to which we had access. This patient recalled fantasies in childhood of a huge and powerful spider-mother about to pounce upon her and kill and devour her.

A mother need not be "angry" and retaliative to harm her daughters. She may be selfish and self-centered, indifferent to her daughter's welfare, unable either to make her feel that she has any value as a girl or that there is anything desirable in growing into womanhood. From the ranks of these women there are recruited some ardent feminists. It is a defense reaction against the repressed and intolerably painful feelings of their inadequacy and worthlessness as women. It is a kind of desperate psychological race. If for a minute they stop thinking and proving to one and all that women are better than men, then from childhood memories there might emerge the unbearable thought that really women are not worth anything.

Unfortunately, in our files there are many examples of psychoneurotic and other adjustment problems in which feminism was a prominent factor. From our abundant material we have selected one case, since with variations of economic, educational, cultural and other details, it is fairly representative. The victim of a family situation, a woman forty-two years old, came to us with a serious anxiety neurosis and a wealth of psychosomatic symptoms located in the genital region. Much repressed material came to light during a long period of treatment. It might well be called, "How to Make A Feminist."

The patient's father, William R., or Bill, as he wished to be called, was a likable chap and successful in his business. However, this was relatively unimportant to him. For one thing he had inherited wealth. There was another and weightier reason. His real vocation in life was remembering his wonderful college athletic record almost fifteen years before. He never forgot, and no one within the sound of his voice at a social gathering ever got a chance to forget, how, by a brilliant end run, he won the football championship for his good old alma mater. In the living room there were cups galore, footballs, medals, ribbons, even the gloves which he wore when he took the intercollegiate boxing championship. He prized his trophies, kept them brightly shining and displayed them to visitors with "modest" comments as to how they were acquired. He could tell you offhand the record-holder of every important varsity event in the last quarter century.

There were four children, Billy, aged ten, already on the waiting list of his father's beloved university. Joan, aged eight, our patient-to-be. She was accepted with disappointment, bravely borne. The next child would be a boy. He was—Jack, seven years old, and then little Jim, almost six.

Bill was a regular pal—with the boys. Never was he too busy to play games with them, to coach them and shape them for the heroic roles he felt sure they would play in college athletics, their natural heritage. (Little Jim let him down. He grew into a bespectacled, not too robust, but a cheerful and happy chap, very studious, who became an archeologist.) Joan tried her best to join with her father and the boys in their activities. Secretly she loved dolls, but the boys made fun of that. As an athlete, Joan was a flop. When she ran forward eagerly with outstretched hands, hoping to catch the ball, which she never did, one of the boys would be sure to yell, "Get a basket." When she fumbled the football, which she always did, she knew what was coming, "Butter fingers, Joan, hang on to it or go back to your dolls." She appealed to her father, first silently with anguished looks, later verbally. He was not much help. True, he did not side with the boys, but about the best he could do was, "Don't tease Joanie, boys. Remember she's a girl." Sometimes Joan retired from the unequal contest in tears. But she was persistent. She adopted the casual sloppy clothes of her brothers and imitated their emphatic manner of speech. She never gave up hope that one day she would get a nod of approval and a pat on the back from her adored father. Her mother was fragile, passive, ineffectual. Her usual contribution was, "Joan, don't talk and act so roughly. Put on your nice silk dress. Be a little lady. Now, get Mamma a cup of tea." Worst of all were the many private conferences between father and her brothers, from which she was excluded. No conferences with her: "Ask your Mother, dear."

Joan pondered. Obviously, she was different from her brothers. Already she had suspected it was an anatomical difference. She confirmed her suspicion when her older brother obligingly showed her. Boys had something she lacked. Here was the magic which unlocked the door of intimacy with her father. She could never be quite sure whether she had ever had it and it had been taken from her, or whether she had never had it. Soon after she began to daydream vividly about being a boy and enjoying the joys and privileges that went with it.

Joan went to boarding school. She neither liked it nor disliked it, though she felt most of the girls were "too fluttery and silly." She participated halfheartedly in the rather mild school athletics. Joan had a short and rather tumultuous crush on one of the women teachers. Later she despised herself for it.

She entered a good women's college, did well enough academically, and graduated without any particular distinctions. She decided to study law and completed the second year of the course. Then, suddenly, she married a fellow student and gave up her studies. "I am not sure why I married. I don't think I was really in love. At least, I *didn't feel excited*. Maybe I was afraid not to marry. Maybe if I didn't then, I never would. I was lucky at that. My husband is a fine and good man. He has put up with a lot from me" . . . "Maybe I quit studying law because somehow I was afraid I wouldn't be able to compete successfully with men." But frequently there were fantasies, detailed daydreams: "Joan R., the brilliant young woman attorney, again scores victory over battery of noted lawyers" . . . "Joan R., well-known woman lawyer, wins important case before U.S. Supreme Court". . . . And Joan became quite an authority on the great women of history. Not offensively so, but she really studied their lives exhaustively and had a splendid library on the subject. Secretly she was thrilled whenever women triumphed over men. Again and again and in many versions she read with delight how the weak-kneed and weak-willed king of France had to bow before Joan of Arc's wisdom and soldierly courage.

Of course, her marriage was not a success, although she did her best. She even pretended to enjoy sexual intercourse, but actually she never experienced "any feeling" until toward the end of the second year of treatment at the age of forty-four. She had two children, a boy and a girl. Her obstetrician thought she was wonderful during labor and bore the pain with the utmost stoicism. Many times during treatment, Joan upbraided herself: "I am afraid I did not want the children much. It was my duty. I never really warmed up to them." Later, "It is better. I am glad to have the children. But it is pretty late."

This is the tragic story of Joan. Treatment helped. She has reclaimed a large area of feminine territory. Her understanding husband stood by nobly. He loves Joan and she comes pretty close to loving him.

What we have said need not disturb parents or send them frantically scurrying to the books or to a psychiatrist. Because Johnnie makes a "face" is no reason to think he is leering at his father and planning to approach his mother sexually. Nor does Mary's secret little smile mean she is plotting to "cut out" her mother and seduce her father. While knowledge is always helpful, yet here it is scarcely necessary to have precise, detailed information. In the average normal home, the several steps leading to adult heterosexual love are taken naturally enough and without too much turmoil. In the normal home, too, the situation is covered and unhappy repercussions and sequels are pretty much discounted, since the respective activities and spheres of interests of the little boy and the little girl are recognized and respected. They are not the same, but they are equally important. "That's my girl," should be spoken as often and as enthusiastically as, "That's my boy." We shall have something more to say, in the chapter entitled "Their Fathers' Daughters."

Chapter X

LESBIANISM—THE BIOLOGICAL AND
PSYCHOLOGICAL TREASON

HOMOSEXUALITY IN WOMEN, or lesbianism, is very ancient. It has been the target of many conflicting opinions and attitudes, and even those who are caught in its web express divergent viewpoints regarding its personal and social implications. Sometimes it is regarded as a physiological problem, sometimes a psychological one, sometimes it is considered and discussed restrictedly as a moral issue. Some homosexuals, supported by a fringe of public opinion and a number of writers, think of homosexuality as an asset, definitely superior to heterosexuality and a hallmark of creative and artistic temperament and genius. A lesbian told us that the mere thought of heterosexual relations filled her with horror and sometimes made her vomit. "It is so filthy and disgusting." More feel trapped and realize the limitations, difficulties and dangers of their situations, but emotionally they shrink from even the contemplation of sex life with the opposite sex. A fair-sized group feels the stirring of heterosexual love. From time to time this usually weak inclination can be strengthened by skillful treatment and something of a sexual metamorphosis can be accomplished.

Of course, homosexuality is a social threat. We doubt that it has increased greatly in ratio volume through the ages, but we feel that when a culture accepts homosexuality and gives it semi-approval or treats it with levity, there is involved a threat to the survival of that culture. Biologically, psychologically and morally, homosexuality is enervating and devitalizing.

It has been said that normally sexed women can unfailingly detect even carefully masked homosexuality, particularly lesbianism, in a social gathering. Perhaps the biological threat to their survival endows them with extrasensory perception, but this is scarcely scientifically provable. Furthermore, in this day when there is so much loose talk about homosexuality and so many misdirected suspicions, it is wise to be cautious. We have heard men indicted as homosexuals because someone saw them looking into the shop windows of an interior decorator or women accused of lesbianism because they had a strong, overhand tennis serve.

Fortunately for us, the agenda of this book permit us to escape discussion of the many complexities and intricacies of homosexuality. Perhaps we will be led into oversimplification. However, we are chiefly interested in those childhood situations, particularly mother-daughter relationships, which conceivably might erect a barrier blocking the attainment of adult heterosexuality and possibly open the door to the substitution of lesbianism. Probably there are a few instances in which homosexuality occurs on a physical basis, an imbalance of the ductless glands. However, by and large, female homosexuality, like its opposite male number, seems to be rooted in psychological damage with the thoughts and feelings it invokes and accumulates largely buried in the unconscious mind, beyond the awareness of its victims. In other words, lesbianism seems to be largely a matter of the psyche, not of the body.

Many causes of lesbianism have been postulated. For instance, the excess of available males in the population. Obviously, not every woman can get her man, especially as some women get more than their share. Then, particularly in large cities, there is loneliness which, combined with economic necessity, leads single women to live together. Then there is the sequence of girlhood crushes on teachers and other older women. Perhaps there is the festering of an unhealed psychic wound, inflicted in childhood by being sexually assaulted or forced into a perversion. It seems to us that these and other things may at most, and it is a small most, stimulate into activity a lesbian nucleus already imbedded into the personality in childhood.

At present, the evidence would seem to indicate that the roots of lesbianism are in undissolved and unfulfilled mother-daughter relationships. Usually there is added a weak, insufficient and inadequate relationship between daughter and father, which is important but secondary. The daughter-mother relationship plays the leading role. The explanation must be given in somewhat schematic and generalized fashion. No one situation is "just like" another one. No two people, no two children, no two girls are exactly alike, either physically or psychologically.

The little girl's femininity is derived basically from her

wish to be like her mother. The wish to be like someone else, and to have his characteristics, is called "identification." Therefore, in order to grow into a woman psychologically as well as physically, to acquire the thoughts and feelings of a woman, the little girl must be able to identify successfully with her mother.

If femininity and womanliness are to be gained, they must be worth the effort. The little girl must see and feel that her mother is worthy of emulation. And more than that. To the child the mother must seem to be important enough and loved enough by others so that there is in sight a worthwhile reward for being like her—a woman. And even more, that women are worthwhile people with an important place in the world and important things to do.

Now, it is well to introduce the role of the father. Roughly, at the ages of four to six, when the little girl's psychological gender is being shaped, she wants to love and be loved by her father. His willingness, ability and desire to accept, value and love her as a girl have much to do with making femininity desirable in her emotional eyes. The role of the father is complementary to that of the mother and good daughter-mother identification can be defeated if the father fails to play his part satisfactorily.

Let us now scrutinize some of the more common factors occurring in the family situation which may interfere with or even totally block the process of identification with the mother, so necessary for the child's future welfare as a woman and for the development of her sexuality.

1. The mother herself may be so masculine in her thinking and sometimes even in appearance and behavior, that

identification with her leads the little girl indirectly to the assumption and display of masculinity rather than femininity.

2. In the normal process of growing up, the little girl not only imitates but also competes with her mother. But for one reason or another, the child may be frightened of her mother and shrink from competition or rivalry with her. In attempting to escape frightening competition, the child may avoid femininity altogether.

3. Rightly or wrongly, the little girl may become imbued with the feeling that she is of small moment in her mother's eyes, that her mother cares very little for her and reserves all her love for the father. Then in her childish logic the answer may seem to be that to be loved by mother, one must be a man, like father.

4. The situation becomes more difficult for the little girl, and reaches an emotional dead end, if and when she turns to her father and finds that he, too, is wanting. He is little concerned about her and brushes her aside. Now begins the frantic quest for love. Since the mother usually is more accessible physically, the child turns to her for the love and security which is not there. At most she finds a few scraps of "love" and emotionally tries to subsist on them. At best, there is apt to be produced not real femininity, or even a reasonable facsimile of it, but merely some female mannerisms with a distrust of the male.

5. As we have indicated, the father can help and, indeed, his help is much needed, in painting the beautiful picture of femininity and budding womanhood. But he may mar the picture or even distort it, so that it becomes a caricature. He may be weak, lacking enough male traits. He may be

indifferent. He may be unpleasant. He may be so with-
drawn from the family life that the little girl finds it point-
less or impossible to love him deeply. Then at her sexual
maturity, the total lack of experience in caring for men,
makes it easy, should the opportunity present, for the
biological drive to be deflected into the channels of lesbianism.

The absence of the father through death or divorce may
produce somewhat the same situation. So, too, may his
long absences on business affairs and when on his occasional
stays at home, he is too tired and preoccupied to give much
attention to his daughter.

6. The family situation may be such that the small
daughter feels devalued and that for her the only thing
that counts is to be a boy. This may be seen in families
where the parents feel and show a decided preference for
the boy children. As we have observed, in families where
there are a number of boys and only one girl, or when
the little girl's playmates are chiefly boys, the boys often
"gang up" and make the girl's life unhappy and undesirable. For this reason persistent, exaggerated and prolonged
tomboyishness comes under suspicion as a factor in the
making of a lesbian. It may indicate dissatisfaction in the
girl with her sex.

Only occasionally is any one of these situations pronounced enough to produce lesbianism. Usually there are
various combinations, sometimes accidental, one reinforcing
the others, and then their united strength may be enough
to reverse the natural developmental processes and produce
the deviation of lesbianism. There is, however, the saving
grace that, even when some of the outlined situations exist,

favorable events may offset them. There may be the leavening effect of mother surrogates, love affairs and sometimes just the right kind of marriage.

We may now illustrate from our files how lesbianism may develop in real life.

Beatrice, a girl of twenty-five, the daughter of a wealthy family and born and brought up in Europe, was sent to us for the treatment of a "highly nervous state" with an overwhelming fear of being alone. For two years she had suffered intensely and when left alone, her panic was so severe that the family had a servant on duty with her around the clock.

At her first visit she related all her symptoms in precise detail. Then there came a long pause, during which there were obvious signs of mounting inner tension. Finally, her eyes brimming with tears, Beatrice burst out with this statement: "You might as well know the truth! I'm a homosexual and I like it. It doesn't bother me a bit and I don't want any treatment for it. You may treat my nervous condition if you like, but it has to be understood that my sex feelings are not to be a subject for discussion." (Consciously, homosexuals rarely come to the psychiatrist to have their sex deviation dealt with concretely. The reason may be some emotional or social crisis. Or they may be intensely jealous of their partners and feel that they are being unfaithful. Or family and friends may be trying to interfere. Or there may be the threat of legal action. Or there may be blackmail.)

In any event, we soothed Beatrice by telling her we would deal first with her nervous symptoms, but that it was only fair to warn her that one condition, in all likelihood, merged into the other. Of course, the tension, the phobias, and the lesbianism were closely entwined.

Beatrice was under treatment for several years. In spite of many discouragements, she was persistent and courageous. Among other things, she said that once she had loved her mother, but in recent years she disliked her thoroughly. For a long time she would not discuss her father. "He is beneath contempt." As successive layers of the psyche were stripped, it was revealed that to the age of six, Beatrice had loved her father tenderly. Her love for him was great enough to condone his failure to reciprocate, his lack of understanding, his indifference. At about this time, the mother went to the hospital to have a baby. There followed two blissful weeks for Beatrice. She waited on her father hand and foot and overlooked his indifference and annoyance. She daydreamed that her mother would die in childbirth and that she would take her place. She would even be the new baby's mother. The day before her mother returned from the hospital, Beatrice confided some of this to her father. "Wouldn't it be wonderful, Daddy, if Mummy died and never came back? Then you and I could be together all the time." The father was horrified. No doubt he felt he had begotten a little monster. He spanked Beatrice soundly, shamed her thoroughly and said, "I could never love a little girl who ever felt that way." From that moment the terrified child turned in a panic to her mother. She tried to expiate her former hostile sentiments and to wipe them out of mind. Her beautiful and tender love for her father turned into bitter scorn and hatred. A few years later when he died, she felt no sorrow, only mild contempt

As a teen-ager, she was attractive to boys, but she fled from their attentions. She adopted masculine habits, manners and dress. At eighteen she fell in love with a girl her own age. Soon the relationship became a physical, sexual one and until she was well into treatment, she was never without a homosexual partner.

During treatment gradually and painfully there came a change in this patient's sexuality. As she worked through her conflicts, interest in homosexuality slowly waned and finally disappeared completely. Men became more interesting socially and personally. At the halfway mark of treatment, she was bisexual—about equally attracted to men and women. Now she is dating steadily with men and thoroughly enjoying it. We would not be surprised if one day soon we had word of her betrothal and soon after that a wedding invitation.

Many years ago, from London, there was sent to us a lovely-looking girl for treatment. In spite of her rather severely cut and tailored clothes, she was feminine in her manner. Although only nineteen years old, her life already had been blasted by two serious homosexual affairs. The first was with an older woman and lasted more than a year. Later, Irene fell deeply in love with a young and beautiful divorced woman. "I never loved anyone, male or female, as much as I loved her."

Instead of mother love in her childhood, there was for Irene a vacuum. Her mother's chief interests were fine clothes, expensive furs and jewelry, and increasing addiction to sleep-producing drugs for which she frequently required sanatorium treatment. The father was a warm, generous man, who loved the children—a brother, two older sisters and Irene. Irene was his favorite and she adored him. Unfortunately, he died when she was twelve years old. When this was discussed with the patient, she acted and talked as if in a stupor. During her childhood, Irene was something of a tomboy and had no great interest in dolls or in feminine activities. In none of the several schools she attended did she realize anything but a small fraction of her considerable intellectual capacities.

After her father's death, Irene never again lived with her mother. Instead, she made her home, by strongly expressed preference, with her father's relatives. One of his sisters, a spinster, "Aunt Jack," was her favorite.

This is the abbreviated story of Irene. No one knows all the ingredients that go into the making of a lesbian. Certainly in this instance the total absence of mother love and the parting by death from the father at the age of twelve, were factors. We believe that we succeeded in reversing the direction of her sexual path in life, but it was a long and painful process.

Nothing we have said in our brief discussion of lesbianism need alarm parents. Given a reasonable amount of mother love, love and understanding from her father, and recognition of the importance of her position *as a girl* in the family circle, it is unlikely that the female child will travel the troubled path of lesbianism later in her life. If, however, there is little or no mother and father love or their substitutes by surrogates, with belittlement of her role as a girl, then there is some danger that she may never find and exercise her true sex function and sink into the lesbian "well of loneliness."

Chapter XI

THE CHILDHOOD VACUUM

IT IS said that nature abhors a vacuum. We presume that the ego of nature is affronted if everything is not in place in its orderly material world. By the same token, psychiatry is affronted and saddened whenever there is a vacuum of love in childhood.

A story is told of a child whose mother was practically a prostitute. Naturally her manifestations of love and affection were sketchy and inconstant, sometimes kisses and caresses, then, if men called, the child was pushed out of the way. One day the child was lost. On a busy downtown street, the little girl stood confused and helpless with tears in her eyes. A lady shopper, motherly and with a way with children, tried to help her. The child only screamed and said, "Go away, go away. I want my mummy." To this child, and to many children, any kind of a mother is better than no mother.

In various places in this book we have cited the long list of maternal and other parental omissions and commissions which create vacuums in the personality of the child where there should be love. Some of these vacuums are produced by catastrophes which may be inevitable—for instance, death.

Adults do not contemplate death with any high degree of pleasure. Various sayings, some serious, like, "In the midst of life we are in death," or, "It's later than you think," or grimly jocular, like, "No use worrying, when your number comes up, then that's it," are designed to dilute the fear of death. Children are not comforted by such philosophies and aphorisms. On the other hand, they are spared the contemplation of the finality of death. The death of a mother falls very heavily upon the hearts and souls of little children. What *can* we say to them? Our best efforts are pathetically bungling and ineffectual. "Mummy had to leave us." And then the child, panic-gripped, "When is she coming back to us, Daddy?" Or, "Mummy is happy now with the angels in heaven and is watching over us." But, the child thinks, "But I can't see her. Why did she leave me?" We wish we could devise a formula to tell children of a mother's death. There is no satisfactory one. Each situation is different. In general, we feel it is advisable to explain the finality of death, as far as it is possible. Or else, some day the curtain of evasion, however shielding at first, will have to be raised. The sad news should be broken in a gentle and tender emotional setting by those whom the child loves and trusts, with accompanying physical expressions of love and affection. Sometimes the father can say in effect, "Children, we all love each other and we will stand together and help each other." Sometimes the father may indicate to the little girl that she can help him as mother did. But, this must be done with thoughtful caution. There is the danger that a chain will be forged which the daughter can never break and no man will ever be able to take her father's place in her life.

In a careful study and thoughtful analysis of very young children in two foundling and nursery homes, deprived of their mothers by death, desertion, etc., René Spitz * presents a moving account of what happens to children when the power line of mother love is cut: In spite of excellent hygienic and sanitary conditions and splendid treatment, the general health of the children was very poor and the mortality high. In an epidemic of measles in eighty-eight children up to two and one-half years old, the death toll was twenty-three, or 26 per cent. This in contrast to the average mortality from measles outside the institution of less than one half of one per cent. It would seem too, that the developmental growth is retarded. In a ward of children ranging from eighteen months to two and one-half years, only two of twenty-six surviving were able to speak a couple of words and walk. Very few could eat alone. None were able to control their bodily functions. While, of course, there are many factors, yet at least the partial conclusion would be that measles and other childhood infections, plus a mother, involve less of a life risk than the infections minus a mother, even though the home conditions and treatment are inferior to those of the found-ling home.

In many of the children in the foundling home there was in the last third of the first year a decided change in

* Spitz, René A.: "Hospitalism. An Inquiry into the Genesis of Psychiatric Conditions in Early Childhood," in *The Psychoanalytic Study of the Child*, Vol. I. International Universities Press, 1945.

the behavior reactions to strangers. The behavior varied from extreme friendliness to generalized anxiety, expressed in blood-curdling screams. Often there was an avoidance of inanimate objects. In the Balinese culture there is a very ancient and very unpleasant tribal custom. A mother nursing an infant at her breast will suddenly snatch her child away, pick up another woman's baby and nurse it. The frustrated babies scream and fight and often become unconscious. The Balinese in adult life do not display much emotion. In the face of even a slight anxiety-producing situation, they are apt to fall into a deep sleep.

Spitz believes that the damage inflicted on foundling-home infants deprived of maternal love, care and stimulation is irreparable. Even after the fifteenth month, and under very favorable physical environmental conditions, the deterioration continues. It would seem that being deprived of a mother, without replacement by emotional warmth from other personal sources, deals a crushing blow to the body and psyche of the child.

At the other extreme of life, old age, it is interesting to note that patients frequently speak of and to their mothers, long since dead. Often they relive childhood scenes with them. Apparently even the destruction of brain tissue by senility and hardening of the arteries often are not able to efface the memory of mother love.

It is just as well that young children deprived of their mothers cannot have a preview of the substitutes in whose care they will be placed. Sometimes it is comforting to see loving hands reaching out to receive them. More often the picture of the procession of relatives, stepmothers, institutions, is frightening.

Not long ago a foreign-born housewife in her thirties, the mother of two children, came to us for help. Since the birth of Ruth's younger child, a daughter nine years old, she has been depressed more or less constantly. Even more upsetting to her are frequent anxiety episodes with distressing panicky feelings, fear of suffocation, palpitation. The mere thought of going out, or of something that must be done, or being alone, precipitates an attack. Usually she can control her anxiety reactions if her husband is close at hand.

It soon became apparent that her experiences in childhood had left their mark on her personality. Ruth is a dependent, self-conscious, tense person, but at the same time she is demanding and querulous. She respects her husband, an easy-going chap, but her perfectionistic tendencies and meticulous housekeeping habits make her critical of him.

Ruth—now a moderately attractive woman—as a child was sickly, pale, puny and homely. Her sisters taunted her because of her homeliness. Between her and her mother there was a strong, two-way attachment. Her mother loved Ruth very much, but not too wisely. She kept her tied too closely, no doubt attempting to compensate for her ill-favored appearance, and both mother and child were unhappy if separated even for a few days. Ruth's father was devoted to his wife and family, loved Ruth more wisely than did the mother and was a source of strength and support.

This was the picture when Ruth was seven years old. Then her mother died of malignancy and a few weeks later her father suffered a fatal heart attack.

For twelve years, until her marriage, Ruth was shunted around from the home of one of her three older married sisters to another. Apparently in each situation a sister kept her until the "Ruth not wanted" attitude reached the saturation level. Then Ruth was passed on to another sister. "I hated every minute of it." Ruth felt unwanted, inferior to her sisters' children, deprived of sufficient money for clothing and even carfare to school. She felt, too, that her sisters, in their attitude toward her, were revenging themselves because she had been her mother's favorite. Ruth married at nineteen, in order to "escape my sisters," but her self-love has prevented anything but a fragmentary participation in her marital sexual life.

Ruth already has lived about half of her life in unhappiness. Certainly the deprivation of mother and father love at the age of seven was a factor. The sisters' giving her a home through a sense of duty and not love, completed the devastation of her personality.

One of our colleagues told us of a dramatic happening in his group-therapy class. A newcomer, a woman, appeared for one of the sessions. Another woman, a member of the class since its beginning, took one look at the stranger, burst into a passion of anger and said she would never attend again if "she" (the newcomer) was admitted. "Why?" "I don't know, but get her out." It developed she saw in this woman a resemblance to an older sister who had cared for her after her mother's death. We are glad to report that after many frictions and verbal battles between these two women, they became close friends. The one became a surrogate upon whom the other worked out her long-stored-up repressions and resentments, dating back to her unhappy childhood experiences with her sister.

We would not want to give the impression that the chances of a motherless child's falling into the hands of a loving surrogate are hopeless. Actually, they are quite good. On our own professional honor roll there is a long list of fathers, grandmothers, stepmothers, sisters, aunts, many others, who have performed a beautiful labor of love for helpless children and given them complete lives. We think we would give priority to the young father whose wife died leaving three young children. His income was limited and he could not afford much help. He worked hard all day, but after work he gave himself to the youngsters, cheerfully and selflessly. Among other things, he would pantomime and mimic and the children would go into peals of laughter as he successively enacted the roles of mother and father, figuratively washing the dishes with one hand and imitating the punch which knocked out the champion with the other.

Sometimes friends and even strangers without blood ties to the children, are God-sent surrogates. Rachel Cooper, * herself childless, was such a mother. "A woman like a strong tree with branches for many birds; tough and enduring in her strength and good sense, yet as warm and embracing as the river itself."

Of course there are vacuums produced even when the mother, far from being dead, is very much alive and in evidence with her daughters, perhaps more than the average mother. When mother love, however lavish be its

---

* From *The Night of the Hunter*, by Davis Grubb, published by Harper & Brothers.

manifestations, is innately selfish, the kind of love that feeds on itself and has as its object complete emotional possessiveness and absorption of the child, then the vacuum is not apparent during childhood, but it emerges glaringly later on in life. This is the main theme of this book.

We say again, a child is always part of its mother. This is so true in babyhood that the baby in some sense still feels physically connected with its mother. If the infant could be confronted with the fact that now it is a separate being and could understand what that means, it would perish psychologically and perhaps physically.

Many physical things that sometimes are wanting, often may be supplied, sometimes almost miraculously. If needed, the endocrine substances, notably thyroid, may transform a gross-featured, slobbering, defective child into a normal youngster. The marvels of heart surgery may change a "blue baby" into one with a properly functioning heart and circulation. But there are no powders or pellets and no surgical instruments which can introduce into the personality of a child something needed above all else—mother love.

It is not only the tie to the mother, but also to the home, since for the little child, the home is the haven of security, the expansion into bricks and mortar of the mother's womb. If a baby does not experience the much-needed satisfaction and sensory satiation of that precious emotional foodstuff, the budding personality may mold itself into any of a number of forms, all dangerous.

Currently, much attention is being given to the study of childhood schizophrenia. Not so many years ago these children often were classed as feeble-minded, even though their

IQs were high and they might have superior intellectual endowments. It is now known that they are mentally sick, they have a psychosis. We do not have nearly enough of the answers to the riddle of childhood schizophrenia. We do not know whether there is something innately in the baby which causes it to withdraw or whether the mother herself holds back. Or both. Some of the mothers are schizophrenic themselves, but not all of them by any means. Many are quite normal and anxious to do a good job for their babies. Some to whom we talked say hesitatingly that the baby, while it clings, does not seem warm and responsive. Therefore, these mothers become nonplussed and anxious and they tend to hold back. This has led to some interesting developments in the treatment of child and adult schizophrenic patients. For want of a better name, it is called direct therapy. In the gospel we are preaching, we are chiefly interested in direct therapy, since it shows how basic is mother love and how difficult and tedious it is to put something into the personality of adults that should have been inculcated so easily and beautifully during their own childhood.

In a general way, psychotherapy is based on the assumption that the patient's illness, as for instance a psychoneurosis, is acquired. The psychiatrist, somewhat analogously to the surgeon, seeks to open an abscess containing psychologically poisonous material consisting of hidden, repressed, distorted emotions. In schizophrenia, there is reason to think the situation is somewhat different. The psychosis does not seem to have been acquired in the sense that a psychoneurosis is developed. There is no abscess to be opened and drained. Rather is there a deficiency, an absence of something needed in childhood, a deprivation of vital needs, a lack of the feeling of the "right to live." Seemingly in very early childhood, infancy, the hunger of love, to receive and to give love, was not satisfied.

The veteran pediatrician, Kisser, who has a deep understanding of psychodynamics, compares the present dilemma of psychiatry in regard to schizophrenia with an earlier mistaken approach by pediatricians to the treatment of rickets. The earlier workers were engaged in an industrious search for an infection in the child with rickets. They were committed to the thesis that all human disease must be caused by the invasion of the body by some poison. Therefore, they failed to cure rickets. It took medicine a long time to understand that sickness may be caused by deprivation, by the absence of something vitally needed, and that its effective treatment might depend upon attempting to supply this vital need which should have been satisfied early in life. For this reason we suggested that the treatment of schizophrenia be thought of as Replacement Therapy.

The significant area of this replacement therapy is the pre-verbal phase, during which the patient tries to satisfy the love-hunger which was not fed during childhood, before the ego was developed. It is blind, instinctive, frightened yearning and reaching out for love and survival. It is inarticulate and symbolic. The usual methods of psychotherapy, reassurance, free association, discussion, scarcely serve to break through the psychotic outer shell. These are more or less adult devices and one might as well speak classical Greek to an aborigine who is making queer, inarticulate noises and going through fantastic contortions.

The aborigine would be frightened. So is the schizophrenic.

In this therapy, particularly during the more or less mute, symbolic, primal-need stage of the patient, the therapist becomes the mother. There is a progressive deepening of the emotional relationship between patient and therapist. This may be expressed by many symbolic gestures, perhaps offering the patient a nursing bottle and the like. The therapist brings to bear the feelings which he perceives as being positive and associated with the potentially good and loving mother. The patient deepens his symbolic involvement with the therapist and increases the emotion he associates with the good mother.

We had not meant to present a small essay on this subject. Nor are we convinced proponents of this plan of treatment. We feel it will undergo many modifications in the future. But we feel, too, there is contained in it a nucleus of dynamic, helpful truth. Our chief object in presenting it is to emphasize again the seriousness of the love vacuum in early life and the danger of its being filled with abnormalities, sickness and emotional sterility in later life.

We feel strongly that a lack of mother love contributes a great deal to the serious problem of delinquency and crime in children in this country. J. Edgar Hoover regards childhood delinquency as our nation's greatest peril. In 1954 there were a million juvenile delinquents and the larger number of crimes were committed by boys and girls and young people who had not yet attained their majority. In the Kingdom of Evils which men have made, Ignorance, Poverty, Crime, Disease and Legal Entanglements may be given high priority. Even in this relatively prosperous land there is still far too much poverty. Poverty and delinquency and crime often are closely linked. Poverty makes for crowded living, dissatisfactions, no real family life, emotional tensions. No wonder boys and girls want to be at home as little as possible. They join up with "gangs" on the streets where there is more space, more companionship and—more danger.

Mental disease, mental defect and delinquency in the mother are potent sources of delinquency and crime in her children, particularly in her daughters. The mother is indifferent and neglectful of her children's welfare and if she is delinquent or criminal, the children, again particularly the daughters, readily imitate her behavior. Important as are all these factors, we believe that in the production of delinquency and crime the highest priority should be given to the absence or inadequacy of mother love.

If one drew a hypothetical psychiatric map, there would scarcely be an area in which the development of psychoses, psychoneuroses, psychopathic states, delinquency and crime was not influenced in some measure by insufficient mother love, either in its vacuums or in selfish over-possessiveness.

There is Johnny Rocco, * a tragic figure with a long record of delinquency and crime:

"The only person in the household Johnny loved was his mother . . . 'But she never favored me. She favored Richie and Davie. Davie—he's dead now—he was her favorite. I was trouble to her. I was always on the outside,' Johnny says heavily. 'When Davie died, she said she wished it was me instead.'

* From *Three Men*, by Jean Evans, published by Alfred A. Knopf, Inc.

"Christmas . . . 'my mother would get my brother Richie something and my brother Davie something, and she'd tell me in advance I wasn't going to get anything.'

"He wanted to make her love and pet him, too, as she did David, but he did not know how. He had a secret way of paying her tribute: 'Money I stole, I would never give to my mother.' He earned a little periodically, selling *True Confessions* magazines. He gave her that money.

"Once he borrowed a shoeshine box, hook-jacked school, and worked from morning till night. 'I made two bucks and a half. Boy, I was hungry, but I wouldn't even buy a roll. I wouldn't even spend something for carfare home. I wanted to give my mother all of it.'

"Johnny would rush home after school and make a great show of sweeping the floors or polishing the stove. He would urge and urge his mother to send him on an errand. Tense and watchful for the extravagant praise he craved, he'd even make overtures to David. But something always happened to burst the bubble; a quarrel with David, a rebuff from his mother—and Johnny, overcome with rage, frustration and self-pity, would swing back to thieving, baiting David, and screaming savagely at his mother."

We fear there are too many Johnny Roccos, many of them in penal institutions, perhaps forever lost to society.

All in all, there is no adequate substitute for mother love.

Anna Freud studied the children bombed out from the slums of London and sent to the country, often to beautiful estates where their physical needs were adequately supplied. These youngsters did not do as well and were not as happy as those who stayed with their mothers in the danger zones. Anna Freud's report about bombed-out children applies to victims of other catastrophes, as for instance the terrible floods which have been sweeping over the United States, and which usually involve temporary separation of children from their mothers.

But there is a separation other than death which is not temporary but permanent. It is adoption.

Adoption may be the saving solution for children who have lost their parents by death, or desertion, or who may be unwanted, often because they are illegitimate. But adopting is by no means sure to cure the sickness of the unloved child. The signing of the adoption papers does not necessarily guarantee a baby's future happiness. There are many obstacles to be cleared. For one thing, there is usually a very long interim between the application for a baby and the actual adoption. No doubt much of this formality and red tape is necessary to protect the interests of the baby, but no doubt, too, much valuable emotional ground is lost, some of which may never be regained. We have not heard this unfortunate situation better described than by Pearl Buck *:

"I first came to know professional social workers through the adoption of four children nearly twenty years ago. My husband and I, loving children, decided to adopt a family, since nature had denied us the joy of children by birth. We went to a reputable agency, made ourselves known, and began the process necessary to prove ourselves good parents. It did not take too long in those days; the

* From "The Touch of Life," by Pearl Buck; *The Atlantic Monthly*, November 1954. From her book, *My Several Worlds*, published by The John Day Company. © 1954 by Pearl S. Buck.

process was courteous and civilized. In due course our big third-floor bedroom became a nursery, but without a nurse, for we wanted to take care of the two lively babies ourselves. A year and a half later they were joined by an equally lively boy and a girl, each a few weeks old.

"In the rich years between the day they came home and today, I have kept myself abreast of developing adoptive practices as well as a layman can, and have taken an active part as a member on the boards of three adoptive agencies. My interest in this subject is far more than personal. I doubt that I am a good mother in the old-fashioned 'mom' sense. I love people from the moment they are born until they die of old age on their way to a hundred. The newborn child is to me first a human being and only second a baby. I am not a peasant mother—that is, not an instinctive one. I do not wish to mother the world. I am not infinitely maternal. But I have deeply enjoyed being a mother to my children.

"Aside from this, my firm belief is that all human creatures deserve a happy childhood as a right and as a prerequisite to normal adulthood, and that the first essential to happiness is love. I have observed that if a child does not have a wholehearted love from and for someone before he is five years old, he is emotionally stunted perhaps for the rest of his life. That is, he is unable to love anyone wholeheartedly and is to that extent deprived of a full life. This loving and beloved person is ideally father or mother or both, but lacking these, a kind-hearted maid or nurse or grandmother will do. It should be someone who has the permanent physical care of him, so that through the daily washing and dressing and feeding and play he feels the pervading and continuing presence of love. It has to be real love. The professional coddling that a trained nurse or attendant gives a baby in a foundling home or hospital does not fool even the baby. It takes more than a clock-watching employee to make a child feel secure.

"It is amazing how discerning a baby can be. A child in the care of a good but unloving foster mother soon sinks into impassivity and begins to fade. Love is the sunshine of his growing soul, and when there is no sun, the soul stops and body and mind begin to lag. That is why children in orphanages and boarding homes look dull and are either too silent or too noisy. Babies used to be kept in hordes in orphanages until it was discovered how quickly they died of nothing at all, apparently. Of course they died for lack of true love.

"What about the professional adoption agencies? Their function is to get children adopted. Alas, they are too often so involved in their professional standards, their lists of questions, their vested interest in the job of the homeless child and impatient adoptive parents, that sometimes I fear more children are prevented from finding homes than are ever placed by them.

"Children ought to go as quickly as possible from natural mother to adoptive parents. Let us admit that sometimes this speed would mean a mistake. Even so, I believe, the total damage would not amount to that which the long delay now causes. There is a fearful lag in the average adoptive agency. Workers put in their eight hours a day faithfully enough, I daresay, but far too much of their time is spent at paper work, filing and red tape. This is made necessary to some extent, I know, by the differing laws of the individual states. A child is often limited to one state or one area in his chances for adoption, each agency serving only one area, without possibility of interchange between areas. Again the child bears the brunt of his sad exclusion. He continues to wait upon laws and professionalism and bureaucracy.

"Many professional social workers know little about children. They do not seem able to see the difference between firm, healthy, muscular flesh and flabby fat. Too many social workers have never married and have no children of their own to teach them. To my thinking, one who works with babies or little children should not be without experience in the daily care of a baby. Even being married is not always enough. There has to be the loving heart.

"The profession is becoming a hiding place for small people, too timid to break petty rules and come out for the great principles of child life. And the greatest of these and the first commandment is love. Everybody who comes near a child, or who influences the life of a child in any way, must be capable of love—a love so generous that every child is dear and every child a valuable treasure.

"The professional in the adoption field has, indeed, a power over human lives which demands a largeness seldom found. She—or he—sits in judgment upon two people, weighing them, examining them, prying into their private lives, and it is this professional who decides whether or not they shall have a baby."

While we are not in complete accord with these views, yet there is a lesson in what Pearl Buck writes. She certainly does understand and appreciate the overwhelming need for love in the early years of life.

It is commonly agreed that the child should be told of the adoption, told in a setting of love and affection. A simple formula is, "We loved you the minute we saw you and we wanted you for our very own baby." If the child is not told, it has no defenses against remarks from playmates and the children in school. Almost never can an adoption be kept secret and it is well that it cannot.

How to answer the questions of children about their blood parents is not easy. The adoptive parents may not know much, which may simplify the problem. There can be no covering formula. Each situation is different. In any event, the parents will cast the best possible light upon the natural parents and the circumstances that led to the adoption.

Illegitimacy? What can be said? We think the less the better. It need not be known. Among the fantasies of children, the daydream of different, wonderful parents, sometimes of noble blood, is not too uncommon or abnormal. Perhaps it is a bit more likely to occur in adopted children.

Adoption presents serious problems for parents, but none of them are insurmountable if the drive for adoption is wanting a baby to love and to prepare for adult life. In the hands of good parents the innumerable details of everyday living need no explicit directions. Perhaps there is one thing. Let them think of themselves and feel themselves the actual parents: "This is our child." So when some behavior problem occurs, as it does with all children, they should be able to avoid the twin pitfalls: "Poor little waif, it is not his fault," or, "We don't even know who her parents were, perhaps something bad that is inherited is beginning to show up." No, a thousand times, No! Simply,

"This is our very own child. We can work out everything with love, understanding and common sense."

This is a good place to express also our firm belief that nurseries in lying-in hospitals are too strictly managed. We are opposed to the rigid separation of mother and child which obtains in many maternity hospitals. Perhaps, the plea of the danger of respiratory diseases and other epidemics has some merit, but, in our opinion, it is not enough to compensate for the psychological loss of depriving a mother of her baby at a time when it is emotionally important for both mother and child and for their futures, together and apart, that they be close to each other physically as much as possible. Never again will there be the same opportunity for mother-child unity. A friend of ours, the wife of a physician, tells with glee how she thwarted the spinster maternity nurse and managed to keep her baby with her for three hours by concealing it. "It was the only chance I had in the hospital of getting to know my own baby."

Chapter XII

THEIR FATHERS' DAUGHTERS

"WE HAVE no ambition to don the mantle of infallibility concerning the relationship of fathers to daughters and to deliver ex-cathedra sermons, "What fathers should know about Their Daughters." Such a mantle would be far too large for us. The father-daughter relationship is one of the really important and often forgotten facts of life. The nature and quality of this relationship makes a tremendous impact upon the personality of the girl and, either directly or indirectly, for weal or for woe, plays a most important role in the shaping of her future life. Yet, surprisingly enough, its significance is commonly misunderstood, belittled or ignored. Even among those fathers who do have some realization of its significance and far-reaching effect, there are still many who disregard it with the plea, "Mary is a girl, I am a man. Her mother knows more about girls than I do. I had better keep out of it." We think it goes without saying that fathers cannot keep out of the lives of their daughters.

The capacity of a small child for an intense, vivid, emotional life is usually minimized, often frankly disbelieved by adults. This is a tribute to the effectiveness of our repressions. By the time we reach adulthood, the picture we retain of our childhood is a curious conglomerate of events imagined, embellished, wished for, with many of the most important things either completely or partially forgotten. This forgetting is not by any means an accidental process. As a general rule, we remember that which is pleasurable and forget those things which are painful. In other words, we tend to protect ourselves from mental discomfort by forgetting those things which upset us—or if this is not possible, by replacing anxiety-producing memories with others which, while they may be disagreeable, are less so than the ones they replace. This process is technically referred to as "repression." Children, as anyone can observe, are able to apply repression with especial ease. As a result of this process, however, adults either lack altogether, or are largely unable to appreciate and understand such things as the father-daughter romance. Such situations are particularly prone to repression for the reason that always the small girl, sooner or later, comes to realize that her love for her father can never bear the fruit of her fantasies. Therefore, even under the best of circumstances, there is always a good deal of disappointment in the feelings of the daughter for her father, with a consequent spur to repression. It is a great pity that this should be so, since our own repressions deprive us as parents of a great deal of that understanding which is so helpful in our relationships with our own children.

The father-daughter romance has its practical aspects, such as the child's imitation, sometimes years later, of her father's various ways of coping with everyday problems.

At the same time, however, it contains much of that precious intangible material of which immortal romances are made. Never again for the girl in the loves of her life and in her marriage will there be an emotional relationship with a man which will not derive many of its markings from the love for her father and his love for her. This will operate for her life happiness and fulfillment, or its unhappiness and fragmentation. There are two vacuums in the early life of a little girl which should be filled by her father.

In the vast army of frustrated women there are, among others, two large groups. There are those women whose intense girlish love, admiration and trust in their fathers were disregarded, ignored and betrayed. Can they ever again care and love deeply? Will they ever again dare to give full love, admiration and trust to a successor—the husband-to-be? Many women, unable to love a man except perhaps very incompletely, have wasted and ruined the lives of potentially fine husbands.

In the second group there was a large measure of love between father and daughter. The father, however, not only had clay feet, but his whole personality was streaked with immaturity. His daughter did not find in him the strength, resourcefulness, intelligence, and wisdom so necessary for the proper support and growth of her love. In the files of psychiatrists, the records of divorce courts and in the hidden mental archives of unhappy women, there are innumerable examples of women capable of loving and trusting, but who, because of lack of knowledge, discrimination and judgment, are wasting away their loves and their lives upon immature, useless men.

As we look at the life histories of our women patients a little more closely, so often we find trails leading back to inadequate and distorted father-daughter relationships. Three types of situation seem to emerge, all of them crippling to the personality and setting very heavy odds against the attainment of happiness, security and fulfillment in adult life. In one group, true enough, there was paternal love, but it was selfish, immature and often sickly, overdone love, unconsciously and sometimes consciously, playing on the dependency of the daughter and enslaving her. Nevertheless, the girl may not face the fact that her great hero, father, does not even nearly approach heroic size and is indeed an emotional weakling, wanting in all those qualities which distinguish a real man. Yet the pygmy outlines of this male caricature are deeply etched into her personality and, unconsciously, in her adult loves she seeks a facsimile of it. Perhaps it is fortunate if she never finds such a man. If she does, then there is another marriage between two adults who are emotionally immature children, destined for chaos. Should she mistake a reasonably mature young man for the father figure and he, perhaps attracted by her unsophistication and childish ways, marries her, then there is in store for him disillusionment and unhappiness, and for her confused groping among emotional realities with which she cannot deal. Marriage is meant to provide nurseries only for children, not for wives.

Or, did the father-daughter relationship tend toward a vacuum in which the traces of love or sometimes, indeed, any kind of relationship, were absent or diminished to the vanishing point? There are women who often say to us in one way or another, "I never really knew my father."

The reasons for this are varied and, to complicate the picture further, we are more apt to see several factors working in combination than to observe any one single factor solely in operation. Some men are very timid by nature. Some are actually frightened of women, for reasons not known even to themselves. Some wives are so aggressive, voluble and overactive that the husband literally cannot get a word in edgewise and is forced willy-nilly to play more or less of a passive role.

Some husbands secretly regret their marriage and though they cannot or will not dissolve it, they show their resentment at being "trapped" by refusing to be really an integral part of the family or to participate actively in any family affairs or relationships.

There is the husband, possibly the commonest of all, who secretly cares very deeply for his family, including his daughter, but who is too inhibited to express his feelings. He would often much like to show his tender or affectionate feelings, but is afraid that to do so would be "sissy," or "unmanly." Needless to say, these unfortunate concepts were themselves formed in childhood from his parental associations.

The other extreme is exemplified by the following story. A woman once said to one of the authors, "Doctor, my father was a violent-tempered drunk. He never entered into the family life in any way except to discipline us like an army drill sergeant. He stood up for what he thought was right, though. I've seen him throw Webster's dictionary right through the window because its definition of a word didn't agree with his. Yes, you had to respect Father, he was *all man!*" This was her mistaken idea of masculinity.

How many readers would agree with her conclusions in regard to this caricature of manhood?

And in the third group there is deep, unconscious hatred of the father. He had not only failed her, but he had repulsed her. Why? Who knows? Perhaps he did not love her because she was not as pretty as her sister Jane. Or as accomplished as Anne. Or perhaps just because she was a girl. In her childhood, eagerly reaching out for father love and acceptance and finding no answer, she almost never judges her father "guilty" at the bar of her childish judgment. She solaces herself with many little excuses: "He has to hurry. He is so busy. He has to work hard. He really does love me very, very much." She *cannot* hate her father. She *must* love him or perish emotionally. So when her father's coldness and disdain force hatred into her soul, she can, and indeed must, repress it, relegate the damning evidence of his indifference to the land of forgetting, the unconscious, and tightly close the doors against its emergence. And, she strives to keep it there by clinging desperately to her father, as if her loving appeals and advances had the magical power of dispelling the gathering clouds of hostility. In this area are some of the most tragic denouements that psychiatrists must witness. Too often in treatment when the nature of her real and deep feelings begins to rise to the surface, the patient is terrified. Such a woman once rushed screaming from our office. Does she really hate her father or his memory? Even such a thought was too horrible to contemplate. Her conscience assails her. Her façade of security begins to crumble. Often she cannot bear it and she flees in a panic back to the false reassurance of her father and the protective, but dangerous, cloak of the neurosis. One thinks of horses led to safety from a burning barn, yet so completely terrified by the fire, smoke and excitement that they break away from their rescuers, rush back into the flames and perish.

We trust we have not viewed with too much alarm and presented the father-daughter relationship as a complicated problem. It is not. Actually, it is quite simple. As a matter of fact, if normal paternal love exists, the situation largely takes care of itself. Of course, some mistakes will be made, but they are of trifling importance and later on will be remembered with amusement by both father and daughter. No general covering formula can be given. There is a basic pattern, but naturally there are individual differences, which suggest modifications.

In the setting of the home there should be ease, warmth, informality. The father is not speaking the lines of a play. He is easily and naturally expressing in his words and manner his love for his daughter and his appreciation of her affection for him.

No two children are alike, except, perhaps, identical twins. Fathers often marvel at the enormous differences in their daughters. Even at an early age Mary may be energetic, outgoing, self-sufficient, seeking and enjoying the company of other children and adults beyond the family circle. Jane is quieter, wants to be at home with her parents, particularly with her father. She likes to be noticed, made much of and makes shy little bids for his attention. Both youngsters are normal and both need the love of their father. Mary seems to need less. From time to time, she may interrupt her activities to go to daddy for a kiss or a pat and then she goes back contentedly to what she has been doing. Seemingly, she just wants to know that daddy is there and loves her. Jane needs the support of more constant and larger doses of demonstrations of love and probably will need it for a longer time. Once on a quiz program, two little girls, each about nine years old, were asked, "Who would you take with you if you had to live on a desert island?" One replied, "Daddy," and then added, "and Mummy." The other child said, "My boy friend." In any event, the thoughtful father will realize that, while there should be no difference in the quantity of his love for his daughters, yet differences in their personalities might suggest shadings of quality and modes of expression.

A surfeit of even a good thing is not good. So may it be with father-daughter love. Its volume may be very large, with many demonstrations of affection, and yet it may be lacking in those qualities which hallmark enduring love. It may be very satisfying for the child at the moment, but from it there may not emerge future confidence and security. It may be selfish, fencing in the father and daughter. Then it does not expand as true loves does, to include others, but, rather, jealously shuts them out. A good father should always keep his feelings and those of his daughter within the bounds of reality. It is cruel to a little girl to encourage her to count on things which cannot be fulfilled except in harmful fantasy. When the child says, "Daddy, when I grow up, will you marry me?", to reply, "Yes, honey, I certainly will. I am your best boy friend," is a mistake. His ego may be flattered by his daughter's proposal and he may enjoy the bit of humorous fantasy, but he forgets the emotional farce is too rich for a small psychic stomach. The little girl is serious, even though he is not. She has proposed marriage to the man she loves and has been accepted. Perhaps the cornerstone for broken trust and later tragic disillusionment has been laid in the mind of the child. True, adult conscious understanding will give the perspectives of actuality, but conscious intelligence rarely effaces completely the deep impress of early emotional experiences.

There is a type of immature husband and father who, having exhausted the possibility of making his wife into his mother, courts his half-grown daughter. Even though it be unconscious, it is none the less psychological incest and it may be as devastating to the personality as is physical incest.

Elizabeth Barrett Browning was indeed fortunate. Her great loce for Robert Browning and his tender, understanding love snatched her from the clutches of a selfish father who tried to possess her, even to using the expedient of furthering the false idea of her hopeless invalidism. Not many women are as fortunate as was Elizabeth Barrett. The vast majority suffer the fate of Daisy M.

Daisy M. was the daughter of a small-town lawyer, only moderately successful. Her parents did not get on well, but they decided to stick it out together. The important factor in the unsatisfactory marriage was that Daisy's father, who had been deeply attached to his own mother, constantly demanded from his wife maternal care, solicitude and "fussing over." He did not want a conjugal partnership. Soon the wife, after a brief maternal response, declined to be her husband's mother, and her behavior made that very plain. By unspoken, but mutual agreement, they terminated their sex life.

Thereupon, the father turned ardently to his daughter. In fact, he referred to Daisy as his "little mother." They became intimate confidantes and, in effect, established a pact which excluded the mother. They agreed that, "Mother does not understand." Daisy babied her father and loved it. Each day she eagerly and anxiously awaited his return from his office. Then hugs and kisses, and the child rushed to get his slippers, give him his aspirin, rub his head or his back, hold his hand. But no less did her father love and pet her. He told her every detail of his day. It was his happiness to satisfy her smallest whim. He bought her expensive toys, later on clothes and parties and trips beyond his income. If there was any hesitancy in giving her what she asked for, Daisy soon discovered that a little pouting or a few tears put into her lap just what she wanted. Besides, it was such fun "making up" with Daddy after a little "tiff."

At his wife's repeated insistence, her husband finally and reluctantly consented to Daisy's marriage to Jim, a nice, reasonably sensible young man she met at college, who had his way to make in life. For a short time it was intriguing to him to coddle and "baby" his attractive young wife. But Jim soon tired of it. Besides, he could not afford to get Daisy one tenth of the things she demanded. "I don't see why you can't. Daddy did." Jim was hard hit when he realized Daisy did not want a baby. With some idea of getting their marriage on a better basis, Jim insisted and finally Daisy became pregnant.

To a psychiatrist who saw her because of "depression,"

it was obvious that she hated the pregnancy and everything connected with it, including Jim and sex in general and particular. Then followed a train of severe functional symptoms—headache, nausea, vomiting, "terrible tiredness," pains and aches "all over." Daisy was cheerful only when she "sadly" expressed the fear that "the doctor will have to take the baby away from me; I am deathly sick." But the doctor finally said, "No abortion." Even now, years later, Jim still winces when he remembers "the hell I went through."

In this instance, psychiatry failed. It was not possible to find any garments of emotional maturity small enough to fit the personality of this child-woman.

The baby was born. Of course, there was a divorce. Now, "happily" enough, Daisy is back in the Midwest with her child, keeping house for her father. Her mother is dead.

While the course of true love does not run smoothly, yet without constancy, there is no true love. Of course, lovers disagree and quarrel, but if they are really in love, there is a margin of safety and they know it will come out all right. Children, and perhaps particularly little girls, do not have any intellectual emotional gauge. They cannot understand and are deeply hurt when their fathers blow hot and then cold. The inconsistent father creates harrowing conflicts in the mind of his small daughter. For a few days when everything goes well at the office, he comes home feeling on the top of the wave. He responds warmly to his child's advances and there is a good relationship between them. Few fathers realize all that this means—

tenderness of love, idealism, complete trust and security, rosy dreams of the future.

Then things go wrong. He loses an important case or his boss is grumpy or a fellow laborer upbraids him for some trifling mistake. Then he comes home. His little girl rushes to meet him with shining eyes and welcoming arms. Without a word of explanation, he snaps out: "Betty, get out of here. Go and play somewhere. Why are you such a nuisance?" The structure of love and reliability he has built in his daughter's mind and heart crashes to the ground. It is little wonder that many little girls, after a long course of such ups and downs, hope-raising and hope-shattering treatment, turn away in disillusionment and frustration from men, perhaps forever, and, perhaps, even seek to punish men in revenge for the wrongs inflicted upon them by their fathers.

It has been said frequently and it is commonly true that parents should settle and compromise their differences about their children in private. Certainly a knock-down and drag-out battle about Mary's untidiness or poor record in school or Jane's "sassiness" in the presence of the children is not edifying and may leave permanent scars on their personalities. But there are exceptions. The father may be timid or he may be acting in the interests of family harmony, yet when he stands by without intervening and sees gross injustice done to his daughter, then he is failing in his duty. His little lady fair is in distress and he does not come to her rescue. He may love her, but he does nothing. He would do more for a strange child on the street who was being abused. We know women whose bitterness and hatred of men wrecked the lives of their children, particularly if, in rage, they think the children preferred their father. A little girl said to us, "If Daddy loves me, why won't he help me?" Why is he silent when a sadistic mother, in the name of discipline, inflicts all sorts of petty cruelties and injustices upon an innocent, helpless little girl? Usually a mother will defend her young against a cruel, abusive father. When the situation is reversed, he has an equally serious obligation and his daughter's stakes in life are equally high. He, who should be the figure of strength and justice, becomes for his daughter, now and ever after, a craven coward.

For every girl we would wish an ordinary, reasonably understanding and wise, but above all loving, father. He would leave his daughter a precious heritage which she would find invaluable in her future life as a wife and mother.

Chapter XIII

"SEEK NOT TO MAKE THEM LIKE YOU"

MANY PARENTS seek to compensate for the disappointments and frustrations of their own lives by attempting to mold the lives of their children into a "I wish I could have been" mold. "I wanted to be a doctor. We couldn't afford it. I had to go to work. I have decided Bill is going to be a doctor." "Mary Jane is going to go to college. I wanted to, but I never got the chance." And so on. On the surface these plans may seem noble. They may involve considerable financial sacrifice, but usually they are unwise and may even end in tragedy. The penalty that often must be paid by the children of the determinedly arranging parents is accumulative. Its full impact is not felt until adult life. But certain token payments usually are exacted in childhood.

The lives of children take place upon a testing field where, in miniature, are played the "give and take" games which have the utmost significance for the future emotional and social development of each child. Children are much more realistic and much less inhibited than adults in their contact with each other. Not yet have they learned

200

much of the dubious art of double talk, a remark aloud for the benefit of the listener and then a silent, inner statement which may not only modify but even contradict what has been said aloud.

In spite of their sometimes outlandish behavior, children are conformists. The group to which they belong insists that its members subscribe to a certain standard ritual in clothes and many other things. The child who cannot conform is pitied or heckled or both. Perhaps the right to be an intelligent nonconformist in adult life must be earned by conforming in childhood. And here there is a strain upon the understanding and reasonable co-operation of parents—a strain for them and for the child. "For children, the voice of parents is the voice of God." Each child constantly needs and uses the emotional strength of its parents to supplement and buttress its own insufficiency and weakness.

No matter how much children like an adult and give him their confidence, we doubt if any grownup is sufficiently child-wise to penetrate all the reasons why "fashions" start in childhood. Names and mystic symbols mysteriously appear in great profusion on girls' raincoats, bobby sox are worn, there are outlandish haircuts and what not. When and where and how did it begin? What does it all mean?

For almost two years the "Ethical Problems" column of a prominent newspaper has staged a battle of letters about clothes, between the "cool cats" and the "squares." Says a "square": "How can you say that tight skirts are real peachy? Don't you 'cats' know they make one look like they were outgrown, but still being worn as a souvenir?

Even those 950's look like a bunch of rags. . . ." But a "cat" retorts, "All the 'cats' are wearing tailored shirts, straight and tight skirts, jerseys or sweaters, and bobby sox or 950's." And so on. We have only the foggiest notion as to the identity of these articles of attire, but it does seem clear enough that in a crowd of "cool cats," a "square" would be beyond the pale, while a "cool cat" would be an unmentionable in the Brahmin caste of "squares."

Some mothers are somewhat too rigid about their daughters' clothes. They are adamant about dressing in neat, dignified and proper fashion. It is understandable enough, but at a certain age it may be a triple threat to her daughter's standing in the community of girl life. Even though the other girls wear them, many mothers cannot bear to see their teen-age daughters garbed in oversized men's shirts, hanging loosely to the knees. We sympathize with the mothers, but we are inclined to think that it is an example of right thinking in the wrong place. Whether or not a man's shirt is suitable for a girl of fourteen is not the main issue. If a girl is compelled to depart too widely from the standards of the "club," she misses something more important than a shirt. Her position in the group is jeopardized. She is a little less secure. Very much needed at this time are patterns of social security and group support. We are not advising a completely permissive attitude on the part of mothers, but we are suggesting reasonable compromises.

Sometimes, indeed often, girls quarrel. Usually the quarrels are not fistic, like their brothers', but at a certain age a little scratching and hair pulling are within the accepted code. More common are "hurts," tears and pouting, mean remarks to other girls, enlistment of sympathy and lining up of allies. Wise mothers more or less stay on the sidelines. Less wise mothers are "right in there" carrying the ball for Mary or Jane, figuratively tucking up their skirts and dashing into the fray. It is unfortunate. A herd of girls may be immature, but they do have a reasonably accurate sense of justice and in the long run manage fairly well. If their mothers take their affairs out of their hands, they are deprived of the lessons to be learned—lessons of experience which will be badly needed ten to twenty years later in life.

From the ranks of those who are not permitted to learn in childhood, there are recruited the Mrs. Joneses who are hurt and angry or who sulk or cry if there is opposition to having the weekly bridge on Wednesday instead of Friday. Likewise, there will be the Mrs. Smiths who are bad-tempered and tearful if some of the other ladies are in favor of the Joneses' plan. The ideas of the contenders may have considerable merit. That is not the question. It is the childish level at which the argument is carried on and the immature behavior that is displayed. In their child-hoods, the mothers of the Mrs. Joneses and Mrs. Smiths of this world did not hesitate to speak in very derogatory terms of the family of Mary Lou, with whom a daughter had quarreled. Now their daughters follow suit. These female children, grown to a woman's physical stature, are not emotionally and socially tall enough to hit anywhere but below the belt. No matter whether the difference of opinion be about a day for the bridge club or the teaching of sex in school or what not, somehow there begins to be circulated quite a little gossip about the leading opponents in the argument. "My dear, I hear Mrs. —— is having a very hard time with the 'change.' I understand at times she is practically out of her mind." Or, "I hope it isn't true that Mrs. ——'s husband is drinking and running around again." Or, "I am told Mrs. ——'s daughter is pretty wild." These women are using the weapons their mothers used in fighting their girlhood battles for them.

We have already considered the mother who is willing, indeed anxious, to give her daughter in marriage, at least on a lend-lease basis. Sometimes this anxiety reflects the fact that as a young woman this mother may have had a fear of missing the marital boat, or perhaps she caught the wrong one. In any event, she becomes the active, even aggressive, Arranger. She watches her daughter's popularity score as worriedly as the major-league club owner scrutinizes the records of his players. "Why don't you have as many dates as Betty? I am sure the boys would like you a lot better if you gave them half a chance. Don't be such a stick-in-the-mud" . . . "Who is taking you to the school dance?" . . . "Oh, I know it's a month off, but someone should have asked you by this time. You will have to put your best foot forward or the other girls will take the fellows from right under your nose" . . . "I saw that nice Roberts boy today and asked him to come to dinner tomorrow night. You know his father is very well off" . . . "You are such a sweet, lovely girl and so intelligent. You could have your pick if you would perk up and exert yourself." So, on and on, without cessation.

The ammunition is freely supplied within the limits of the family purse, in fact, usually beyond its sensible capacity. There are elaborate parties and beautiful dresses, far too sophisticated. It is an artificial maturity, dangerously anticipating and discounting real and natural maturity, which can only be accomplished by taking one step after another as they are taken in the normal, progressive relationship between children.

Lucy's mother in her girlhood was good-looking and had average intelligence. But she feared she would not be able to compete with a beautiful, brilliant sister, one year older. Indeed, it is possible that this sister did annex for herself a very fine marital prospect. In any event, Lucy's mother was worried. Lucy in her early teens was in the "grub" stage—tall for her age, awkward and gangling. She was neither unintelligent, nor abnormally shy, but she did not seek many contacts with boys. She was pleasant with them, but was chiefly interested in her schoolwork and she had an excellent record. But Lucy's mother was worried and she saw to it that Lucy's father was worried, too. They had wealth and she began a publicity campaign—beautiful dresses, expensive fur jackets, sheer stockings, sophisticated cosmetics and perfumes, modish hairdos. She urged her daughter to "step out," scolded and belittled her when she failed to do so.

Two years passed. Lucy was now seventeen. The "grub" metamorphosed into a beautiful butterfly. Nature, rather than cosmetics and dresses, made her beautiful. But her behavior was not beautiful. Lucy needed only to observe another girl's interest in a boy and immediately she added that boy to her rapidly growing list of male victims. As she blossomed into womanhood, the influence and repercussions of her mother's attitude when she was a child, now drove her to the conquest of young men, as relentlessly as Nina, in O'Neill's *Strange Interlude* was driven by the memory of her dead lover to enslave men sexually.

Of course, the girls in Lucy's crowd are through with her, just as the women she may come to know later in her life will soon be through with her. The girls she knows describe her in various terms, none of them flattering. A few speak of her as "predatory"; others refer to her as a "she wolf"; one girl, who probably has a realistic mother, captions her with a one-syllable, five-letter Anglo-Saxon word.

What made Lucy's mother ruin her daughter's life? Among other things there were the unconscious repercussions of the fear of losing out in her own childhood and the rekindling of her girlhood sense of inferiority. She wanted Lucy to be as she would have liked to be. What made Lucy behave so outrageously? Her mother left open only one path for her inferiority—the siren path of illegitimate psychological compensation. And that brings us to a brief consideration of inferiority reactions and how *not* to deal with them in children, particularly girls.

Probably owing to high-pressured propaganda, many people either do not know or have forgotten how serious is a real sense of inferiority. Radio and TV commentators treat it very lightly and assuredly as something that can be readily corrected by wearing so and so's suits; using such and such tooth paste, razor, hair tonic, depilatory, BO chaser; attending this or that "charm" school and what not. Actually, an inferiority complex is not so easily corrected. It has broken the psychological backs of many men and women. True enough, a little inferiority feeling is a healthy leavening in the personality. Browning called it "the spark that disturbs our clod." It is an effective antidote against blatant and boring self-sufficiency. It makes us less likely to recline in smug self-satisfaction and stimulates us to reach out beyond our poor selves. However, a little inferiority feeling goes a long way. More than a little mires us in our own belittlement; impedes our progress in life in all directions and may reduce us to the level of emotional and social zombies.

An individual may be aware of his inferiority feelings and their causes. Then, he himself may take steps to overcome them. More likely is it that the victim is only partly aware of his inferiority feelings, suffering the dissatisfactions and emotional pains of their stirrings and with some vague realization of their origin. Most frequently the individual is unaware of the inferiority feelings. This explains the behavior of some people who overcompensate for their inner insufficiency by arrogant superiority and sweeping expressions of complete confidence. These are the people who know everything from next year's winner of the world series to every last and gruesome detail of the A and H bombs. And they can do anything from fixing a leaking kitchen faucet to writing an infallible formula for enduring peace.

Many factors may influence the development of inferiority feelings. They may be physical. In girls we have often encountered tallness, obesity, acne, even the normal enlargement of the breasts and the onset of the menstrual periods. A chance remark by another girl about her looks or figure may start a devastating inferiority reaction.

Often inferiority reactions are born of mental conflict

due to all sorts of situations—unhappy homes, poverty, divorce, alcoholism in a parent, indeed anything that shames the child in the eyes of its companions. We have found rather often that if in the home of an immigrant only a foreign language is spoken and perhaps old-world national or orthodox religious customs are observed, the children feel ashamed with their American playmates. At the other end of the scale, it is not easy to live in the shadow of greatness, and an intellectually brilliant father or mother may condition an inferiority reaction in their children.

A potent source of crippling inferiority reactions in youngsters is the enthusiastic but ill-advised stirring of the mixing-pot of childhood relations by unwise mothers. Wiser mothers, if they detect signs of inner belittlement in their children, handle the situation much more sensibly. They may decide it is not too serious and that the youngsters will work it out themselves with perhaps a little encouragement and judicious praise. The immature mother jumps in enthusiastically. Since she is more of a taking than a giving person, her activities, seemingly directed to helping an inferior child, actually tend to affix the child more closely to herself, rather than freeing it, so that it can strive to overcome its inadequacies. Unconsciously the immature mother seeks to make the child like unto herself.

We have seen the same mistakes repeated time after time. Sometimes ill-founded superiority reactions and behavior are induced on the basis of money, family, position, clothes, anything at all, even to the possession of a thoroughbred Pekinese dog. The child reaching out for relief from the tormenting inadequacy feelings and struggling for a "place in the sun," seizes upon anything promising relief. He or she begins to boast and strut. The crowd sets the "stuck-up" back on his psychological rear and the youngster is farther down on the inferiority scale than before.

Sometimes immature mothers initiate and encourage "specialized" attitudes in children. It may be playing the French horn, or philosophy or poetry. In girls it is often ballet dancing, not as a nice accomplishment, which it is, but as a deadly serious and time-consuming business. It does not matter that socially awkward and not very popular Dorothy's school marks drop lower and lower. Nothing must be allowed to interfere with the ballet lessons and practice. There is no longer time enough for the usual social contacts with other girls and boys, so vital for maturing. For a brief period all is well. The clouds of inferiority feeling are dispelled by the sunshine of the ballet and the attention and praise of the mother. But ballet dancing, or anything else, is not the answer. Later in life, usually too late, Dorothy will have to try to learn the bitter lesson that the ability to do odd and special things, "parlor tricks," will not satisfy the requirements of mature everyday living as a wife and mother, which insist on first doing the daily, often commonplace, job.

We hope we have not given the impression that genuine talent and even genius cannot exist in childhood or that if it can and does occur it should be disregarded. In practically every area, and notably in acting, music, painting and literature, our world has been much enriched by the development of talent and genius which first showed themselves early in life. It is doubtful that pure genius can be repressed. By its very nature the divine spark will burst into flame in spite of discouragement and obstacles. But both talent and genius are apt to come to earlier flowering and more complete fruition if encouraged in childhood.

What shall the mother and the father do who think they see in a daughter decided evidence of an important talent? It is fair to warn them that statistically the chances are that it is a false alarm. But it may be real and very precious. There are experts in every field, music, art, acting, the sciences, who are willing to give an opinion if properly approached. Parents should be warned that there are many pseudo-experts, down to the level of unscrupulous charlatans who will give an enthusiastic verdict, hoping to profit by teaching the child.

Let us suppose that a sound, expert opinion declares there is real talent or even genius in a little girl. Then certainly the child should be given the opportunity to develop her ability, even though some financial sacrifice is involved. But other children in the family should not be deprived of what they need and have a right to expect. There are many organizations and foundations which are willing to assist in the development of genuine talent. So far, so good. While time will be needed for instruction and practice, there should be as little dislocation of the school, play and social routines as possible. The expression of the talent in adult life will be all the more satisfactory if the actress, musician or painter has been given the opportunity in childhood of developing not only her talent, but also of maturing her personality. Two brief case reports may illustrate how important it is to make wise decisions.

Sally M., now about forty years old, is in a public mental hospital with a hopeless form of schizophrenia. Ophelia-like, she wanders about the ward pathetically singing a few words. In her early teens Sally had a nice little singing voice. Her mother conceived the idea that her daughter was destined to be the world's greatest soprano. The opinion of a well-known music master was sought. He said, no, never would Sally's voice develop into more than something which might pleasantly entertain her friends. Another expert gave a similar verdict. Sally's mother made the rounds until she found a so-called "master," who said Sally's voice showed wonderful promise and he would teach her. He did. For years. Much money which could be ill afforded was spent. The family was deprived, sometimes, of necessities. Sally's emotional and social growth were sacrificed to "The Voice." Then came the fateful day. With the expenditure of a large sum of money a public concert was arranged. It was a "flop." The few critics who gave it any notice at all turned thumbs down. It was the end of Sally's career.

In contrast there is Marie B. In her field she is so famous and so much in the public eye that it would not be fair to identify her work. Suffice it to say that she has brought surcease from the cares of their daily lives to many thousands. In her girlhood she was tall and gangling. Even though her face was well formed and intelligent, she had a devastating sense of inferiority because "I am as tall as a man." She was socially very self-conscious and awkward and stayed much alone and daydreamed. But from time to time there were manifestations of a certain talent first revealed by pantomime and mimicry. Her intelligent, sensible mother, who was rather anxious about Marie, thought it was worth following. She obtained several expert opinions and the verdict was that Marie had a genuine gift. The mother saw that Marie was given the opportunity to be properly trained. As her talent expanded and with the wise help of her mother, her personality opened and she became friendly, social, happy. As testimony to emotional adjustment she is not only at the peak of her career, but is happily married and has two children.

We cannot overemphasize the fact that there is a tragic finality about childhood. It is important that the emotional and social lessons be learned then and there. If they are not assimilated by a child from its relations with other children, then either they will not be available at all in adult life, or else they will be acquired only in great travail, with much suffering and after many defeats.

One does not need a crystal globe to see that the present tense world situation cannot endure. "Cold wars," "cold peace," nations bristling with armaments, A bombs, H bombs—waiting, waiting in dread expectancy for the fangs and claws of the beasts of war to be bared and civilization to be torn into pieces, perhaps never again to be put together. No, this is not the answer. There is an answer. Unfortunately, it is not an immediate answer. The answer is love—"love one another." It is the only answer and it can be learned only in childhood.

As was pointed out in *Their Mothers' Sons*, the current social profile of man is very incomplete. Were it even half-way finished, the world would scarcely have embroiled itself in two bloody and destructive wars within the short space of twenty-five years and now be threatened by another. Much time must elapse, many additions must be made to the profile and many parts of it must be erased, before man can really be labeled homo sapiens.

The capacity to live democratically and constructively can be acquired only in childhood. Only reasonably mature parents, and particularly mothers, are competent to teach children these democratic lessons and permit them to practice them in their relations with other children.

Man will, without question, always cling to powerful self-protective and assertive behavior drives. The all-important part played by self-preservation in the battle for survival throughout history and pre-history precludes any other possibility. Usually well covered by cultural and ethical layers, there are still cruel and ruthless drives in our species. As time marched on, however, the stark reality of "me and only me," was in some measure diluted by the security resulting from the greater strength of number of human beings, banded together for a common purpose, usually protective. Much later the conscience emerged to influence man's behavior and thinking. Conscience forces a man to stand apart and examine his own behavior. His higher intelligence enables—indeed obliges—him to do so. If his conduct does not measure up to what he thinks it should be or what he would like it to be, he undergoes feelings of guilt and remorse. This is the human conscience. It is still weak and too easily muted. When men act in groups (as in war or mob actions), each individual tends to merge himself into the identity of his leader, thereby reducing his feelings of a personal guilt and stilling his conscience, whether in illegal murder (lynching) or legalized and socially acceptable murder (war). The leader assumes the lion's share of responsibility, while the individual escapes the direct barrage of his conscience. Quite often, nevertheless, the superego, or conscience, stimulates man to rise above his baser self and act in a manner, at once unselfish and self-sacrificing. The annals of catastrophes in war and in civilian life are bright with sacrifice for others, even the sacrifice of life so that others might live. It is promising. We think the day will come when human conscience, ethics, the spiritual man, his soul, will be strong enough to vanquish his unconscious bestial drives.

In the majority of men there is at least a trace (too often only a trace) of feeling for all men, not so much in general, but feeling for each man as a human being, a common ground of sameness under the skin which is the foundation of a true brotherhood of man. Yet, undeniably, even in the best and most mature men and women, the veneer of internationalism is still very thin and patchy. Internationally we are social pygmies—isolationists at heart.

Indeed, even for short distances our social perspectives are quite limited. We would like to cite a few examples from *Their Mothers' Sons*. For instance, if we live on the Atlantic seaboard, we are only mildly concerned by the news of a terrific storm on the West Coast, with loss of life and enormous property damage, or a destructive "twister" in the Midwest, unless a member of the family lives or is visiting in one of those areas or we own property there; but we become much more emotionally disturbed as we listen with rapt attention to a radio broadcast of storm signals on the Atlantic Coast. During a very hot summer in the city in which we live, something went wrong with the water system and the water supply was shut off from one area of the city. Practically every person who mentioned it said in effect, "I am glad we don't live in that section." About one in five added as an afterthought that, "in this boiling weather it must be rather bad for the people who live there."

A little child was stricken with severe polio. A mother who is a good neighbor and had a little boy the same age as the stricken child, was genuinely sorry, but her first thought naturally enough was, "Thank God it wasn't little Jackie." She even had a passing thought of which she was later ashamed, of being glad it wasn't the boy across the street with whom Jackie played so nicely. Then she thought of the sick boy and his distressed parents and gave her sympathy and help.

All this is natural and human. However, it does indicate that the milk of human kindness is first strained through the separators of self, of family, of home and of nation and then what comes through for suffering humanity in distant places is pretty much skim milk. We are troubled when we read in the papers or see on the screen the hunger and suffering of other people, but we are not troubled very long. The next day we may be quite vociferous against reducing the tariff on some article of import. "Certainly not, it might lower our standard of living." It might, but so little it would not be noticeable. It would raise our standard of decent concern for others whose very subsistence is at stake.

Often children in their communion with each other are amazingly altruistic. When misfortune, sickness or death strikes the family of one of their playmates, children may give examples of practical understanding and sympathy which sometimes shame the clumsy efforts of adults. They may propose very thoughtful solutions to their mothers. If there is sickness in Mary Lou's house and her mother is worn out with overwork and worry, it may be suggested that "we have" Mary Lou's little brother and sister "stay with us for a while." Or, perhaps, "Sally's mother is terribly sick" and only a part-time nurse could be secured, "Mother, I won't be home for dinner. We are taking turns looking after Sally's mother and it is my turn this afternoon and evening."

The altruism of children divides itself into two categories: that promoted by various organizations (put a penny a day in this box for the poor), and that which is more or less spontaneous with the children themselves, though it is likely to have its roots in the attitude of a mother who is a good neighbor. The second is much more significant for the social and ethical development of youngsters.

Usually, mothers are not adverse to general altruism, like saving pennies for displaced, abandoned children: "The poor things don't even know there are homes like ours." Or, making up Christmas baskets for poor children: "I couldn't bear it if you children didn't have a perfect Christmas."

When it comes to more personal things, like being nice and decently companionable to a child in school who is of a different color, immature mothers are apt to be very dubious. "After all, darling, he [or she] is so very different. He won't understand and will take advantage of your kindness. I am sure the families of your best friends won't like it. I wish you wouldn't." Although it may be quite a distance away, nevertheless this is on the same road of ignorance, prejudice and intolerance as are those cesspools where children are taught to be suspicious of and to hate "them foreigners." "Them foreigners" may live only a quarter of a mile down the road and are alien only in wearing the clothes they brought with them from Europe, in their accent, which they are rapidly trying to correct, and in their religion. Yet, the attitude is, "Don't you children have no truck with them dirty foreigners. Keep away from them."

Generally, mature mothers give more leeway and have a longer perspective. We know a Japanese painter who is either a genius or very close to it. His art is recognized by noted institutions and by fellow artists. He is not even interested in the many opportunities to commercialize his art. He paints only what he wants to paint. Consequently he subsists on the smallest of pittances.

He was bewildered by the war. Probably he was about sixty years old and had come to this country as a child. He had lost all contact with Japan. The FBI cleared him and allowed him reasonable leeway, but naturally, he was the recipient of a certain amount of unfriendly attention.

A lady who had known him for many years offered him the shelter of her home, to eat and sleep there, do his painting there and in fact be a member of the family whenever he wished. Her two half-grown daughters were a bit squeamish about it at first. Apparently they had encountered some criticism in the community in which they lived. Their mother made a little explanation, not too much, and carried on naturally and easily, as though it were a commonplace and everyday procedure. The Japanese fitted into the home unobtrusively. Among the thanks he shyly offered were beautifully done sketches of home scenes, the family and friends, the dog and the cats. The sketches were an unfailing source of joy to the son of the house, serving in the South Pacific. Soon the daughters accepted

the arrangement and were enthusiastic and happy in participating in it. We believe that the international social stature
of these children has grown appreciably.

All in all, the sons and daughters of those mothers who
have some feeling for human beings, no matter who they
are or where they may be, will come through their childhood with a much higher potential for becoming citizens of
the world, than will the children of selfish, immature mothers. Some time, and in the not too distant future, such
world citizens will be of vital import. Again there is a
threat of a world war, which this time might easily mean
the destruction of our civilization and culture and plunge
us into the darkness of barbarism. Those adults who, as
children, were led at least in the direction of the brotherhood of man, will be the human bulwarks against the on-
slaughts of unreason and immature thinking.

A few human beings have far-seeing vision and are
actuated by love for their fellow men. They often suffer
disdain and persecution, but future generations will call
them blessed. Some men are almost without feeling or
conscience for their fellow men. The majority of us are
myopic in our humanitarian vision. But more of us are
coming to realize our shortcomings and striving to correct
them. We will succeed only partially. But at least let us
gain enough understanding so that we do not visit our
limited world perspectives upon our children and seek to
make them like us. In many ways we have failed miserably.
Let us, and particularly let mothers, give children a better
and braver world in which to live.

Chapter XIV

A MOTHER-DAUGHTER DESIGN

READERS OF *Their Mothers' Sons* will remember the chapter, "Design for Childhood." It set forth not the theory but the fact of psychological potentials. These psychological potentials are buds ready to flower and expand and produce a healthy, sound, enduring personality, provided they can find suitable nutriment and stimulation in the environmental soil. But the psychological potentials take what they can get. It was pointed out that if they cannot find suitable nourishment and encouragement, they will be blighted, and an unhealthy, unbalanced personality will result. It will be recalled, too, that the more important psychological potentials were: motion, imitation, suggestibility, curiosity, love of power, savagery, and romancing. The pattern remains much the same and is repeated here. However, in *Their Mothers' Sons* the emphasis and application were particularly on boys. In this book we have focused upon girls. There are notable differences. The mother is of the same sex as the daughters. She has lived as a girl and there has emerged an experience pattern. The mother may know much about boys, her sons, but about her daughters she not only knows but *feels*.

The mother is in danger of following one of two paths, neither one good. Her own girlhood may have been satisfactory and happy and unconsciously she may insistently fit her daughter into her own mold. But times change and personalities are different. Liberal allowances must be made. Then there is the mother whose girlhood was unhappy. She may readily fall into the trap of overprotecting her daughter and attempting to shield her from every adverse environmental wind. In so doing she unconsciously *possesses* her daughter and deprives her of the opportunity of developing an independent, self-sustaining personality. As in most areas of the mother-daughter relationship, the middle-of-the-road policy is the better. From the sum total of girlhood experiences certain things have survival value— love, the emotional warmth of a happy home, some responsibilities and duties in the family life, a reasonable amount of guidance. These the mother can give her daughter.

For those who have not read *Their Mothers' Sons* and who despair in the face of difficult behavior on the part of their daughters, we recommend the careful study of this chapter and the one following. We believe there *is* something that can be done about it.

Admittedly, much of our behavior, even our everyday behavior, is derived from that inner sanctum of our psyches, the content of which is hidden from our consciousness—the unconscious, the land of the unaware. Human logic, of which we boast so proudly, is not nearly of the heroic size that we imagine it is. Much of the reason for what we do— why we marry blondes instead of brunettes, or vice versa, or become doctors instead of lawyers, criminals instead of good citizens, for instance—is not in careful, logical thinking and planning, but comes from the drive of material stored in the unconscious during childhood. However, it would be naive to assert that human behavior is not modified by intelligence, judgment and choice. And much pressure in determining our behavior comes from the environment—the opportunities it offers for the development of a sound personality, but also the opportunities of which the growing child is deprived. Thus is the human personality shaped.

For a long time we have been fascinated with the theory of potentials for development. It seems reasonable enough on the physical side. At first, when the baby-to-be is in the womb of the mother, there are buds of organs, liver, spleen, heart, lungs, what not, hard to distinguish one from the other except by an expert. They seem to have the power to select what they need to grow into complex, highly differentiated organs and parts. But they do not have the power to reject what is harmful, as for instance, the germs of syphilis, tuberculosis, and their growth may be threatened with deficiencies, malformations and disease— even death. After birth, the baby is still very incomplete. It needs to complete its nervous system and to add hair, teeth and many other things. Its potentials reach out for what they need to complete normal growth—food, sunshine, fresh air, exercise, etc. If it finds these things in the environment, well and good, and there is produced a person physically capable of making his way in the world of adults. If it does not find what it needs in reasonable quantity and quality, then the growth is apt to be ill-favored and stunted. Much effort and attention will be needed to put this defective human machinery into such condition that it will function satisfactorily. And the effort of reconditioning may be only partially successful. Sometimes it fails.

Just as there are physical potentials for growth and development, so, too, are there psychological buds or potentials, although they are not as well defined. They, too, reach out into the environment for food. And they, too, absorb and use what they are given, good or bad, beneficial or harmful. These things are woven into a personality and some trace of them will remain throughout life, for weal or woe.

Don't Fence Me In. Motion, physical motion, usually is thought of as a physiological attribute. True enough, it is that, completing the development of the nervous system, strengthening the muscles, etc. But motion is much more than that. Its psychological value is enormous. It is a travel ticket into the outside world, where wonderful and useful things await discovery and experiences are to be gained and stored up, without which life would be meaningless and survival doubtful. It is probable that a child never permitted to move about would be mentally defective. On its tours of discovery, the baby finds out the difference between soft and hard, smooth and rough, cold and warm, many other things. And it bumps into other human beings.

Sometimes we hear mothers boast that their children are good, because they are quiet. "She is a good girl. She stays put. She doesn't get into mischief." Such a baby is not good. Psychologically it is bad. Probably if babies could express their needs and desires, next to food, they would demand the right to move about, to crawl and to walk.

René Spitz writes tellingly of the sad fate of children in foundling homes condemned to solitary confinement in their cots. "The restriction of psychic capacity is not a temporary phenomenon. It is . . . a progressive process. How much this deterioration could have been arrested if the children were taken out of the institution at the end of the first year, is an open question. The fact that they remain in the foundling home, probably furthers this progressive process. By the end of the second year, the Developmental Quotient sinks to 45, which corresponds to a mental age of approximately ten months, and would qualify these children as imbeciles."

We know a young mother who, until recently, was "afraid" to let her sixteen-month-old daughter out of her play pen. She feared the child would fall and she conjured up all sorts of nightmares—brain concussion, fractures, and what not. We persuaded her to let the child move out into the wide open spaces of the room first, then the house. A study of the personality of this mother made it clear that unconsciously she feared not physical injury, but separation from her child. Her husband was overseas and she had not seen him for two years.

We do not wish to belabor the point, but it does seem to us that immature mothers observe the moving child with more anxiety than is normal; supervise it with more personal concern; tend to circumscribe and limit it more closely. We cannot help feeling that the phase of her child's beginning physical activity sounds a warning note somewhere within her inner recesses—an unconscious voice says, "Better be careful, your child is growing up, beginning to move away from you." It symbolizes, and in miniature is, the forerunner of the threatened and total emancipation of the child later on.

All mothers call back their babies from their crawling expeditions. We think there is a subtle difference in the "Come back to me" call of mothers. In effect the real mother says, "Come back to me, baby, so that I may help and teach you to go farther away from me." Says the immature mother: "Come back to me, so that I may bind you more closely and teach you never to leave me."

Even in these days of unrestricted physical activity for females, blessedly freed of the multiple petticoats, pantaloons and other armaments of their great-grandmothers, there are still mothers who feel there should be a difference in the amount and kind of physical activity allowed to boy and girl babies. After all, it is all right, they think, for the little fellow to kick and pummel and make journeys into the territory of the hall or adjoining rooms. The male of the species will have to be more energetic and active. But the little girl: should she not be restrained? Otherwise, is there not the danger that she will develop into a hoydenish and unladylike woman? No, there is not this danger. As a baby, the female needs activity and freedom of motion as much as the male. See that she gets it.

Perhaps one may think of the mother in her close contact with her baby daughter as encouraging and directing the crawling and walking stage and a good deal beyond that. Perhaps to the father there may be entrusted the more energetic physical activities, games and mild sports. But not to the point of making a girl athlete. Dolls, especially dolls that walk and talk and wet, are more important for the little girl's future than baseballs or footballs.

"For Children the Voice of the Parents Is The Voice of God." Imitation. Several times we have referred to the twin-powered driving force of identification and idealization which motivates the imitation of the parents by children. Particularly early in their lives when they are pitifully weak and insecure, they literally live by virtue of the emotional strength they can borrow from their parents, at first largely from their mothers. The more freely they can identify with, become a part of their parents, the more of the vital emotional strength they will be able to find. It will be a long time before the psychological umbilical cord is severed. And so should it be. And the higher the parents stand in the estimation of their children, the greater the confidence and security the children will feel.

Imitation is fluid. It readily flows into channels that are opened to it. Our native language is called the "mother tongue," because we acquire it through a process of imitation. The child hears certain sounds—at first meaningless—from its mother. Gradually these sounds become associated with certain ensuing happenings. "Baby is hungry," and the nursing bottle is produced. "Mummy loves her baby," then kisses and caresses. Thus the spoken words take on meaning for the child. Words are learned one by one. Then they are put together into childish but meaningful phrases.

Striking examples of the power of imitation are evidenced by a child's natural play life. There was probably never a day when little girls did not make use of anything at hand to create a dress and then parade around among their friends in direct emulation of their mothers. Children, in playing house, indiscriminately bring to life all the virtues and foibles of their parents. Parents could learn a great deal about themselves if they could eavesdrop on their children's games. The mother might be quite alarmed to overhear the play "mother," her little daughter, hiss excitedly to her play "maid," when the doorbell "rings," "Marie, if that's that stupid Mrs. Brown, tell her I'm out. I can't put up with that silly old fuss-budget." And one could be pretty sure from this episode, which one of us witnessed, that Jane's mother was rather immature. Jane, who was being teased by another little girl, rushed into the outstretched arms of her sister, the play "mother," who caressed her and consoled her with these words: "Never mind, darling, Jennie Smith is a nasty, dirty brat."

Trite, but true, is the saying, "Actions speak louder than words." Platitudinous admonitions and hypocritical mouthings, however nicely put, will not serve. There is needed the firm and convincing tone of good behavior by example.

Mrs. S. was a stickler for the truth. At least hearing her talk one would certainly think so. Frequently she delivered well-phrased sermonettes about the virtues of telling the truth and the sinfulness of deceit. If her two little daughters lied, she punished them. Yet ever so often, before the father returned home from work, there was a full dress rehearsal, the mother saying to the two little girls, "Don't tell your father this," "Don't mention about so and so to your father," and so on. And when it concerned Uncle Bill, her brother, it was emphatic, "Don't you dare tell your father Uncle Bill stopped in today." Uncle Bill was a mildly alcoholic, ne'er-do-well drone. Mrs. S.'s husband was quite allergic to him, first because he didn't like him, second, because he had often borrowed money from him which he never repaid. But Mrs. S. fed him, gave him money which was needed for household expenses, and, if no money was available, she was not averse to looking the other way when Uncle Bill purloined something pawnable from the house. Soon the little girls began to wink at each other psychologically when mother delivered her admonitions about truth-telling.

"What shall we give children to imitate?" is a tempting question, since it might easily lead to the delivery of a sermon. We do not wish to preach. However, the question must not be left unanswered. If parents and others who have to do with children were asked what they want to give children physically, there would not be any great trouble about the answer. In effect they would say, "We would want to save our children from the tragedy of the weakling. We would want to send them out into life straight, healthy and strong. Therefore, we would see to it that in their childhood they were given the right physical conditions of life." And the psychological parallel is obvious. If we wish to start the personalities of children in the right direction and prepare them for the important emotional issues in life, then we must provide material to imitate which will make them emotionally self-sustaining. The home surroundings of children should contain in liberal amounts those ingredients and qualities the imitation of which may be counted upon to build sound, mature, enduring personalities—honesty, straightforwardness, truthfulness, courage, reflection, judgment, decision, patriotism, tolerance, and, perhaps, at least the outlines of a pattern of service to the community and the nation. And, since the world has become much more compact and accessible, at least some stirrings of internationalism—a striving toward the ideal of a brotherhood of man. It seems like a large order, but these are only some of the specifications for fashioning a participating citizen of the nation and of the world. Equally important is it that the early environment of children at least be relatively free from the opposites of these character-building attributes. In dishonesty, furtiveness, venal lying, cravenness, ill-founded judgment, hasty action and indecision, intolerance, selfish lack of patriotism, disregard of community and national needs and a vacuum where there should be some feelings of international responsibility, we find the characteristics of those parasites who are working so arduously to subvert the foundations of democracy. An appropriate device for children to imitate might pattern itself after a formula for daily living in which there exists at least a rational equilibrium between taking and giving; between accepting favors and fulfilling obligations. Here, indeed, is a pattern well worth the weaving. Of course, it will be imperfect. There will be many dropped stitches, loose ends, patches and "runners." But even crude imitations of the ideal design are very much needed in the imperiled world in which we live.

In order to get a composite picture of what is dangerous for mothers to give their children, and particularly their daughters, to imitate, we need only trace back the silver cords that bind children to possessive, immature mothers. In their behavior these mothers present for imitation unwise, dangerous and sometimes psychologically lethal patterns. There is the "Manager" mother who stifles self-decision and discounts the chances for grown-up thinking, feeling and acting. There is the "No trouble" mother who habitu-ates her children to life in an unreal world, where everything is done for one, and one need not turn a hand for others. There is the professionally "Frail" mother who sacrifices the future of her children, and notably of her daughters, at the altar of her own selfish demands, leaving them in an arid emotional desert in life, or perhaps, if the opportunity is afforded, they put into practice what they have learned and sacrifice others whom they can hold and dominate. The "Don't You Dare Punish My Child" mother insulates one or more of her children against responsibility for behavior and devalues self-discipline. The picture she paints, if imitated by her children, not only leaves them at the mercy of an exacting world later on in life, but makes it likely that they—chiefly her daughters—will follow the same pattern with their children. The gentle, soft-spoken "Pollyanna" mother, however good her intentions, unfortunately presents to her children for them to copy in their lives, a utopian, unreal dream which a very realistic world will rudely shatter. The "Pretty Addlepate," however lovely and amusing she may be, nevertheless, leads her children to overvalue feminine pulchritude and her daughters are apt to indoctrinate their own daughters into the artistry of beauty and give them little else that is more enduring. If her children imitate the "Pseudo-intellectual," then they in turn will foster scatterbrain daughters who dip a little here and there and never come up with anything that is really halfway intelligent and lasting.

In our experience, probably because they are of the same sex and in such intimate association, the most dangerous mother pattern which daughters are the most likely to imitate, is an unhealthy sex pattern. Sadly, too often it is a pattern of sly deceit, sex given grudgingly and for its "trade-in" value. Or it may be a pattern of prudery giving rise to inhibitions and taboos which block the completion of sex life and the realization of its ideals. Havoc is the word to describe what happens to the sex development and sexual lives of many of these daughters of sexually unadjusted mothers.

One cannot sort out the qualities of personality which the daughter should derive by imitation respectively from the mother and from the father. Some of them should come from both. Perhaps one thinks of neatness, good manners and graciousness, gentleness and compassion and womanliness as particularly derived from the mother and, perhaps, strength, resourcefulness and long-distance planning from the father. But do not let either mother or father refrain from contributing whatever they can whenever the opportunity offers.

Make no mistake about it! Imitation is a powerful pestle for mixing in the mortar of childhood, the ingredients which go into personality-making. Even though children may seem to defy the pattern set by good parents and behave in direct opposition to it, yet, later in life, it is very likely that some of the patterns will be repeated, sometimes directly, sometimes in camouflaged fashion.

"*I Know What They Mean By That.*" Suggestibility. Suggestibility is a wide-open channel, through which a considerable part of what happens in their surroundings flows into the personality-molds of children. Suggestibility is an impetus, or inclination, given toward this or that kind of behavior pattern. It is like imitation in that the source and drive of suggestibility is the emotional omnipotence of parents and their surrogates. But it is much more subtle than imitation. Imitation is simple and straightforward. A child sees an adult do something. That "something," however trivial, becomes impressive and worth copying, because of the great emotional influence the adult has over the life of the child. The child tries to imitate exactly what it has seen.

Suggestibility has not the tangibility or directness of imitation. A behavior cue emerges from the environment; more than likely the cue will produce responsive behavior. All human beings are suggestible and notably so, are primitive savages and children. All normal children literally absorb suggestions of all kinds from parents, the family life, playmates and, indeed, from everyone with whom they come into contact. Numerous behavior reactions are produced and, in some shape or fashion, they become a part of the developing personalities.

When a little girl, while trying to be helpful, trips and breaks a dish, her mother may say, "Poor Ruth, she is so nervous, just like her father." The mother, of course, is simply suggesting nervousness to her child. If she persists along these lines, there is an excellent chance that Ruth *will* become a nervous child and later a nervous woman. Then she may break things more important than teacups—perhaps the emotional equilibrium of her own children.

Perhaps we have been unfortunate, but we have seen a large number of children, particularly young girls, who have formed the habit of focusing on the body and its processes by suggestibility from neurasthenic mothers. Sometimes we think of these mothers as "achers" and "ouchers." Mrs. T. is a good, though extreme, example. She is about thirty-five years old, and repeated examinations demonstrate that she is in good physical condition. But her days generally begin with an ache, usually a headache, often a "blinding" one. Pains and frightening sensations punctuate her day and edify the neighbors. Her eleven-year-old daughter, on returning from school, is likely to be greeted by "sick" mother with an icebag on her head, or a hot water bottle at her back and a clinical thermometer in her mouth. Dramatic variations are the discovery of "lumps" in various parts of the anatomy, chiefly in the breast. Never has there been a bona fide lump and once the "lump" proved to be a metal piece on her brassière. The function of the bowels provides a wealth of material for frequent verbal observations. The relative merits of diet, exercises, laxatives, etc., in achieving the much-desired boon of "regularity," are often discussed at length. Little Pat, the daughter, knows entirely too much about physiology and already is beginning to discover fanciful pathology in her perfect little body.

This child's neurasthenia was suggested by the mother. Now Pat is directly imitative. Usually these situations are less tangible. The neurasthenia, or whatever else it may be, is "concealed" from the child, but the behavior and the elaborate precautions to keep it "secret" and "suffer silently," have the hallmark of unmistakable suggestion. The little girl imbibes the suggestion of the thermometer, the ice bag, the hot-water bottle, the array of medicines and the paraphernalia of neurotic illness as quickly as she does the use of cosmetics, and in their way they are just as fascinating.

By way of agreeable contrast, we know a decidedly neurasthenic mother who, with the help of a psychiatrist, is making a fine effort to overcome her difficulty. She has three fine youngsters and almost never by word or look has she suggested her illness to them. They are healthy, robust children with the usual normal disregard of their physical processes.

Through suggestion children may gain or fail to gain the same helpful attributes of personality that are acquired by imitation. And through unwise suggestion their personalities may be burdened with harmful and even crippling personality traits.

Suggestion is a psychological weapon of great strength and usefulness in helping to shape the personalities of children. It is a flexible and double-edged weapon. It should be used boldly to add worthwhile traits to character; and it should feint away skillfully from the undesirable.

Chapter XV

Queen For A Day. Love of power. We feel that all sane men and women, in some small degree at least, desire the approval of their fellow men, enjoy their applause and prize their place in the sun. In all of us there is a love of power and it normally arises in childhood. The childhood love of power is a more or less unconscious wish to dominate the surroundings and to turn them to one's service and pleasure. As grownups we should not have any difficulty in understanding it, since most of us carry some part of the childhood power pattern and drive into our adult lives. Sometimes consciously, usually unconsciously, we love power and we are apt to cling, sometimes desperately, to the few shreds of it we have gained in life. Perhaps this is why the one-man dog is so highly prized. No matter how sorry-looking a mongrel he may be, his master knows that he can count on him for unfailing homage. Few of us willingly relinquish power. It has such pleasing emotional appurtenances. Great prima donnas and actors make innumerable "farewell" appearances. It is even necessary to fix a retiring age for professors, even for professors of psychiatry.

It all begins in childhood. Usually everything is done to keep baby comfortable, satisfied, happy. The baby does not have to be an infant prodigy to learn that a certain sound, called "crying," is very likely to cause the adults in the house to start fussing and rushing about frantically. Perhaps it is something the baby wants removed, a pin sticking into it, or the grimacing face of an overly enthusiastic visitor. Incidentally, babies are apt to be frightened by visitors. One of our colleagues feels that visitors in some way constitute a threat to the baby that it is to be separated from its mother, and he advises that infants not have many visitors. Perhaps, too, the baby wants to be close to its mother since she is not only a source of strength, but often, too, a willing slave.

We feel the baby is entitled to its brief reign of power. The period of dominance is short. Perhaps all too soon the little kingdom is liquidated. Inevitably there comes the sad disillusionment. The phase of happy, irresponsible power over others comes to an end. Annoying, uncomfortable clothing must be worn. Fingers, which the baby's remote ancestors used for feeding themselves and which the baby finds most satisfactory not only for feeding, but also for smearing, must be relinquished in favor of awkward table implements. Uncomfortable and often frightening contraptions, "potties" and toilets, have to be used. Indeed, if one does not use them, one is shamed, often publicly. Property belonging to others must be respected: "Don't touch," "Don't break," "Naughty baby." The child must learn the painful lesson that other adults and even other children have rights and these rights must be respected and frequently conceded. Ultimately each child faces the conflict between the opposition and demands made by her social environment, at first symbolized by the mother, the father and the family group, and the desire to hold or later recapture the power of infancy.

Do not let the curtain which separates the baby's dominance from concession to the social code come down too abruptly and do not let it be an iron curtain. Let there be at least a few peepholes in it.

Serious psychological complications often ensue after grave childhood illnesses, such as rheumatic fever or one of the childhood infections, with complications or any one of many things. A period of convalescence follows recovery from the ailment. The child who has endured the sickness so quietly and courageously now becomes a veritable terror. The parents do everything in their power to make up to the child all the pain and discomfort it has suffered. The youngster, in effect, becomes boss of the household. The merest fancy becomes a command. It is a rare child who can resist the lure of relapsing into the golden days of babyhood, of regaining the power which it once enjoyed. Mishandling of this situation can leave a deep scar on the child's future life; it demands painstaking and careful management. Not too abrupt, strict and stern in denying the child's requests, even though they are a bit unreasonable; not so permissive that the normal progress toward maturity is hopelessly bogged down.

How to handle this critical stage of development? For one thing, it should never be underlined by an excess of attention. Extreme courses of action are doomed to failure.

Undue severity can lead to the child's being abruptly, at times cruelly, brought to the realization of the hard fact that its days of dominance are over. Strict discipline is meted out at the slightest indication that the child is trying to recapture the infant world, with all the power that goes with it. We know of many beaten and terrified adults who, as children, underwent this extreme treatment, which resulted in their twisted personalities. Another example might be that of the person who inflicts the mistreatment he received in childhood on society in general, and whose attitude becomes one of antisocial and forbidding agitation. It may well be that, among the dictators who recently imperiled the whole future of civilization, there were several who, through sadistic behavior and a total lack of humanity, were wreaking their vengeance on society as payment for the harsh punishment inflicted on them by their parents during childhood.

The opposite pole in dealing with the power-drive in children is to spoil them. Misguided and questionably "kind" parents may allow children to hold on to their babyhood power for too long. This too-permissive attitude is often rationalized and cloaked in pseudo-scientific authority by the explanation that it is dangerous to interfere in any way with children's "expressing" themselves. Sometimes one parent or the other continues an only child or a favorite child in this artificial and unrealistic position well into the teens and even longer. The other children always have to give in. Sometimes husband or wife is forced by the other partner to concede—or else. Then comes the day of reckoning, when, as an adult, the spoiled child must face life as it is. It is too late. The individual does not know how to conform. The habit pattern has been too deeply etched into the personality to be erased. There are ineffectual stabs at gaining the spotlight but the audience is indifferent, even distant and skeptical. If the adult attempts to use the weapons of childhood, he may encounter active resistance and retaliation. As was pointed out in *Their Mothers' Sons*, the final result is often a bitterly disillusioned exit from the world of adult emotional relationships, or at best the learning over a long period of time, and in a sad and trying way, the lesson of not only taking, but also giving—a lesson that could have been learned with far less difficulty during childhood.

We have witnessed power-drives in the home by the wife and mother and its unhappy effect upon daughters.

One woman who as a child had lived in a home where her father was completely dominated by her mother, came to us asking that we help free her from the tyranny which she in her own home exercised over her husband. But another woman from a similar childhood environment was afraid of her husband, who dominated her unmercifully.

There are various types. There is the virago, the tongue-lashing, venomous wife. Her husband has only a beggar's choice. He can try for a divorce—and leave the children stranded. He can fight it out, but the odds are against him. He can become afraid and cowed, testing each word before he utters it, lest it erupt the volcano. At best, he may hope to attain a nirvana of indifference, outwardly rendering lip-service acquiesence.

More common than verbal and sometimes even physical methods of dominance are more subtle ones. Any attempt to interpose a block in the wife's having her way, results—

perhaps not immediately, but some time later on—in retaliatory measures, tears, sulking, sullenness, periods of silence, "sadness," not eating at meals, being "sick," what not. "What is wrong, darling?" Long silence. Then a deep sigh —"Oh, nothing." Then contrition on the part of the husband, for something "unkind" he may not even know he did or said.

All this is psychologically poisonous to daughters. They may duplicate the domineering pattern in their own adult lives or they may become passive and abject, unable to sustain their proper role in any grown-up emotional relationship.

Every mother gambles with her children and particularly with her daughters in the game of retention of baby power. The little girl sees only the table stakes, the wish to remain in the position of babyhood dominance. She cannot see the real stakes of future adjustment, maturity and happiness. The real mother is at a disadvantage. In the eyes of her little daughter her bids are low. She offers remote things, not yet of any value in the eyes of the child—the ability at some time in the future to live life unhandicapped, on even terms with other grown-up men and women. The present power is much more attractive. How can the child know it is only a bauble?

With an unconscious eye on lifelong emotional possessiveness, the immature mother plays her blue chips lavishly. On the surface the child is an easy winner. Her mother yields to her almost all of the pleasant, carefree dominance of her baby days. As she gaily rakes in her winnings, a "queen for a day," she knows naught of the future and cares less. It will be a long time before she misses the few chips that mom retains after each hand is played. These chips are the real stakes. They represent the emotional hold of mom on her daughter and, increasingly, they decrease the chances that the little girl will ever attain maturity. Finally, mom has all the chips and her daughter is so deeply in debt to her emotionally that it is unlikely that in her marriage and, indeed, in any adult relationship, she will be able to escape personal and social emotional bankruptcy.

Curiosity. Curiosity may have killed the cat, but it was a significant factor in the survival of our species. Primitive man, threatened on all sides by prehistoric monsters and the awesome forces of nature, became not only frightened and enraged, but also curious as to how these threats and dangers operated. This led to rough, immediate safeguards, then gradually to long-distance planning and protection and, finally, to man's dominance over his environment. However, we still have a long way to go.

Children and scientists have one thing in common. They are both intensely curious. Science is applied curiosity. The dyed-in-the-wool scientist is as pryingly inquisitive as a child, but the scientist has a background of highly specialized information that gives purposeful direction to the eternal questioning in his mind. Beyond that, just like a child, he takes things apart and puts them together to find out what makes them tick. For many of the benefits of modern life, from lifesaving wonder drugs like penicillin, to useful kitchen and bathroom gadgets, we are indebted to curiosity. When one of the authors was a medical student, he was required only to memorize the list of moulds and yeasts and recite them. The professor said they were not important. Students would still be parroting the names if some men, driven by curiosity, had not examined these odd growths, taken them apart and eventually found out that they were very useful. For the A- and H-bombs we are indebted to scientists who were curious to find out whether the atom could be split. At present it is still a dubious blessing, but unless man destroys himself with this knowledge, nuclear fission and its products eventually will be the greatest boon curiosity has ever conferred upon mankind. In fumbling fashion, psychiatry does something similar. It attempts to take apart the personality of a sick person, find out what went into its making during childhood and, if possible, supply what is needed to make it work better. And, eventually, it hopes to apply what it learns to all people, sick or well.

The curiosity of children is backed by enormous driving force. We have little comfort to offer the tired father, home from his work and encountering a barrage of questions from his children. Unless he wishes to lose his reputation for omniscience, he must be prepared to make some kind of answers to such simple questions as these: "Why doesn't our dog purr like kitty, instead of barking?"; "Are big pickles the fathers and mothers of little pickles?"; or, "How is the baby Mummy has inside going to get out?"

Questions like these and many others are not answered in the schoolroom. The best and most natural place for the verbal question box is in the home. The curiosity of children must and should be satisfied. The questions of younger children should be answered simply, directly, truthfully. Authoritative source material should be at hand for older children. At first, "Let us look it up together." Later, "You look it up. Let me know what you find out."

The structure of the growing personality gains great strength in the acquisition of knowledge through personal initiative.

At first the questions of little boys and girls are much the same. Then they diverge; the boys want to know from fathers about sports, planes, war and other "man" things. And the girl begins to go to her mother with questions about dresses, "falsies," the secrets of feminine beauty and, of course, if the home is right, questions about sex.

Even in this modern day, some parents still balk at the manifestations of sex curiosity in their children. Ordinary curiosity, "Yes, of course, that's natural enough." But why should innocent little children want to know about sex? Why should sex-curiosity be so much deeper and stronger than other kinds of curiosity? The parent is horrified when his "nice" little boy ask about his sex organs and those of his little sister. Should he be discovered examining them, the parent may feel he has produced a monster.

Not long ago an enterprising reporter discovered a little boy, *seven years old*, who had been in common jail in California for twelve days for having put his hand under a little girl's dress. It was thought the prison sentence would deter him from "a lewd and immoral life"!

The reason why youngsters are so curious about sex is so simple that it should be obvious. It is a twofold reason. Sex is strong, instinctual, demanding. Naturally, it emerges early in the child's life. Another reason is a stupidly fabricated one supplied by some adults. Sex is shrouded in darkness. Should a group of ladies be talking about sex, which they sometimes do, and the little daughter of the house wanders into the room, there is enacted a remarkable scene.

A sudden silence and wild gesticulating greet the uninvited guest. There is a hush-hush atmosphere thick enough to cut. Then Mrs. Jones makes the usual asinine remark about "little pitchers" having "big ears." Then Mrs. Smith chirps brightly that the weather is humid for this time of the year. Seemingly there is complete and abysmal ignorance as to a very obvious fact—curiosity thwarted and made difficult of satisfaction is at once redoubled. The ladies have forgotten the story of Bluebeard's wife.

What should be done about sex-curiosity? In the chapter on sex, we tried to picture what we feel is a good attitude of the mother toward her growing daughters—verbally and in her general demeanor and behavior. We are somewhat distrustful of formal sex lectures to groups of children. A natural receptive home atmosphere is more fruitful. If it is right, then children do not hesitate to ask questions about sex, and solid foundations for useful and helpful sex information are laid. There is no more important environmental heritage that can be given to children. We repeat again that in the countless "nervous breakdowns" of adult life, one theme that runs through them all is ignorance, misinformation and bad sex-habit formation.

Many sources of sex information are readily obtainable, some of them suitable for children. The comparative sex life of plants and animals, household pets, visits to the zoo, a few good books are excellent means for the instruction of the child.

Opportunities for informal talks with children about sex should be welcomed, but not pressured. Chats of this kind will grow from simple to complex as the children grow older and will be of increasing assistance in guiding the child. And such discussions at the right time and place from sensible, loving parents will reap enormous rewards in emotional health, security and happiness.

In the role of "Information Please" on the forum of sex curiosity in children, the thoroughgoing mother has definite advantages over the immature one. The immature mother operates under several handicaps. Perhaps she is immature because she herself had an immature mother. Frequently, immature mothers have entered adult life ignorant of the nature and beauty of sex. They are likely to be fearful of it and to have developed a long list of personal taboos. Often they are prudish. When a mother speaks of sex as "nasty" or "dirty," one may be reasonably sure she has not grown up emotionally. Usually when these women refer to sex, they mean the sex act exclusively and they are apt to hint darkly, or even openly assert that "it" is the only thing men want from women. Unless she is willing to learn, and apply what she learns, then naturally enough if a woman is an immature mother by reason of a scurvy trick played upon her by her early environment, then there is little she can give her children that is helpful. Sadly enough, she can—and often does—transfer to them her ignorance, fear and prudery. On the other hand, because she is a real mother, the chances are that she has had a more normal and complete sex life than the immature mother. The real mother is a thoroughgoing woman, who does not belittle sex and she strives to make her sex life as full and as noble as circumstances permit. Obviously she is a much better sex mentor for her children than one whose sex experiences have been abortive and fragmentary.

Of course, it takes two people, a husband and wife, complementing each other, to attain the summits of sex. Even though a woman is every inch a woman and a mother, still she may have been sexually defrauded by an immature partner in life. Even complete women are not immune to sexual thwartings and frustrations, but immature women are more liable to them since emotionally they do not measure up to the requirements of adult sexual life. In any event, it is tragic that any mother should visit her sexual mistakes and disappointments upon her children. Every child is entitled to a fair start from scratch in the somewhat hazardous game of sex.

Abortive Little Savages and Small Female Munchausens. Savagery and Romancing. Once females were as savage as their primitive mates and sometimes still are, but largely our culture has left only vestiges of savage behavior in little girls. True enough, it has not been eradicated. Fairly frequently one hears and reads of girls' gangs in large cities, attacking each other with knives and broken, jagged bottles, battling sometimes to the death. Not all the fangs have been drawn, nor all the claws blunted. And at a less dangerous level, there are many "tomboy" girls. A little of this is good and it may fit more or less into the family pattern, particularly if there are brothers. As we have said, it is not good if the girl becomes a wild little tomboy to attract her father's attention and to save herself from being excluded from the father-boys' family club. More natural and better for her future are dolls for the little girl. In her teens, to a considerable degree, the tomboy has been supplanted by the "bobby-soxer" who screams and swoons at the sound of "The Voice." All in all, in our culture savagery is the psychological territory of boys—

noise, rough language, spitting fighting, and the superman and space man.

What is savagery? It is in distilled form, the recapitulation of the era of primitive savagery, the long and bloody trail traveled by our species on its way toward our present plane of civilization. Many individuals have gained at least a precarious hold on the plateau of nonviolence toward each other as individuals, yet tragically, in the aggregate as nations at war, there is more savage bloodletting than in the day of the cave man.

Regardless of its beginnings, it is obvious that children, particularly boys, often act like little savages. It is important to find an outlet for this normal phase of emotional growth. Here is a perfect chance to teach love of nature and self-sufficiency, to stockpile reserves of health and strength, so vital to later life.

There is no reason on earth why an abbreviated program of physical activity is not equally good for girls. They, too, need fresh air and sunshine, games and sports, competition in moderation. There is such a thing as being too feminine. We are compounded of both male and female elements. A hundred per cent male or female would be grotesque. Fortunately, in our culture there is little place for the languishing Lydias of the Victorian era.

If, as is true, there are still primitive residuals in the female, then little girls need normal outlets for them. The finest and best outlets are in the preparation for the physical activities of marriage, childbearing and homemaking. The true mother will help the little girl prepare for her role in life and skillfully block such qualities as slyness, overcoyness, harmful gossiping, deception and evasive tricks, so often and so mistakenly considered hallmarks of femininity.

An untruth is not always a lie.

Romancing, as we use the term, means the telling of untruths that are not falsehoods. The flowering of the imagination has its roots in romancing, among other things. Children, not having the check of many intellectual criteria, will often contrive stories which would make the Paul Bunyan tales models of veracity. Romancing should never be cruelly stifled. The parent who tells his child, "That is a lie, and you are a liar," is in grave danger of smothering or twisting something of great potential beauty, which is only starting to show itself. Truthfulness can be imparted to children with tact and care over a period of time. The romancing phase can be an excellent springboard for launching the child into the world of great romantic literature, which, in turn, provides outlets and rewards for the speedily developing imagination.

An in-between policy is most effective in coping with a child's romancing. A good mother will neither gush her approval and praise, nor will she be openly amused or contemptuous. It is possible that from childhood romancing may emerge that intangible, gossamer stuff which produces great verse, but mothers are less likely than moms to jump to the conclusion that there is a genius in the house. No one will deny that great liars outnumber great poets. Nevertheless mothers should not be overly dubious about the wild and romantic tales their children tell them. It is not likely that children really expect their stories to be swallowed whole. They do want, and actually need, a receptive audience which will not deride or deflate them.

Usually mother can be counted on to be such an audience, a friendly, first-night critic. The wise mother realizes that youthful "make-believe" must have an outlet. There is a risk of a surplus of indiscriminate and overabundant day-dreaming in the world of fantasy if this normal outlet is repulsed too abruptly and deprived of its means of expression. The mother should, of course, keep a watchful eye on the need for impressing the virtues of truthfulness on the child, as she listens to its tales of fancy. She should become adroit in leading a child to the realization that a good story remains good even if we don't "make believe" that it actually took place. In the matter of the romancing of their children, immature mothers are seldom middle-of-the-roaders. They tend to veer too much to one side or the other. We think that some part of their attitude depends upon whether or not they have a prominent role in the romance. If they are the heroines, they seem willing to have it continued as a long serial story. However, if they are excluded, they are likely to remember the demands of truth. Immature mothers are not enthusiastic about their children's having private lives. It is too ominous for the future.

Before leaving these psychological potentials, we would like to discuss the emergence of heterosexual interest and "puppy love." In general, little girls move toward emotional maturity more quickly than little boys. Often this is seen strikingly in groups of boys and girls of about the same age. The social sense of the girls stands out in marked contrast to the awkwardness and gaucherie of the boys. One can see in miniature the reaching out for heterosexual social contacts by the young female, while the males tend to hang back, to cluster together as if for protection, each youngster trying to bolster up his courage to mix with the girls.

More usual than not, there is in little girls, even in those only three or four years old, the sporadic and rather primitive emergence of romantic ideas. Daddy, or possibly an older brother, is likely to be the target for Cupid's childish arrows. Toward her father there may be a protective attitude, wanting to sit in his lap, helping to get his sandwich ready, fetching his pipe and slippers. She is apt to take an older brother's part in his arguments with a playmate or console him in almost grown-up womanly fashion if he has suffered some rebuff or defeat. At an early age, such attitudes of course are only transient, at least in their visible form; but they are indicators of deeper currents that are beginning to stir in the little girl's psyche.

Later, say between five and eight, these attitudes take more realistic shapes in keeping with growing intelligence and experience. A little girl may pretend that mummy has gone away and that *she* will take her place with daddy. From her play-acting, it is obvious that she imagines herself doing the job far better than her mother. In family arguments, too, the little girl is quick to see mother's every little fault, magnify it and take her father's part.

Still later, in school with much contact with boys and girls, there are often transitory crushes on little boys in her class. The romance flowers quickly. Susie, aged seven, confined to bed with chicken pox, was visited by a little boy from her class who had the disease a few weeks before. The little girl, seemingly too sick to be interested in anything, perked up amazingly when the little boy was announced. She combed her hair carefully, put in a bright ribbon, demanded her best bed jacket. Shamelessly she "made eyes" and conversed in honey-dripping tones. Often these romances fade as quickly as they have flowered. Three days later, when Susie saw Ronnie again, they quarreled and she has had no use for him since.

In a later stage of development we find the girl of high-school age ripe for puppy love affairs and "crushes" on various male teachers.

Puppy Love deserves very careful consideration. It is a mixture of fantasy and realism. The fantasy is very rich. Often it is inarticulate, sometimes it is verbally expressed. Two young lovers may sit for hours, hand in hand, building elaborate castles in the air which could not possibly be supported by the foundations of everyday living. It is a beautiful exercise in romantic imagination. But sometimes abruptly the fantasy may break into stark reality and there may be a tragedy. We think the outcome depends to a considerable degree on how the adults in the family circle, the father and very particularly the mother, regard and manage the puppy love. It is one of the acid tests of parenthood, notably of motherhood. Parents usually do not take puppy love seriously enough or, on the other hand, they take it too seriously. When Jack says to his mother, as he nibbles one of her biscuits, "Mother, you ought to get Mary Jane's mother's recipe for biscuits, they are wonderful," or when her daughter Cathy remarks, "Mother, why don't you wear brighter colors? Bill's mother has the spiffiest peppermint-stick dress. She is just about your age," the mother should not dismiss the whole business in a flash of resentment, saying, "If you think they are so perfect, why don't you move in with them?" There is more to it than that.

It may be "puppy," but teen-age love is real and serious. Recently there have been some suicide pacts between boys and girls—shockingly concluded. In other cases, they have run off and the girl has returned pregnant. We think that these disasters may happen because the parents take the affair too lightly or too seriously. In the former instance, the youngsters may become determined to show the adults they mean business. "They had better stop laughing at us and making those sarcastic cracks." To adopt a superior attitude and completely ignore their love may produce the same result. On the other hand, rigid, tyrannical measures are no more successful. "Lock Jane in her room until she comes to her senses." "Don't let Mary go out of the house alone." "Send Susie to visit her aunt in Kalamazoo." "Put Ellen in a school where they will watch her every minute." These suppressive measures usually fail. From time immemorial youthful lovers have defied authority and often circumvented it. And they still do.

For the parents, who should know how serious puppy love can be, the middle-of-the-road policy is the wisest and safest. The mother is interested, not scornful or too humorous about it. She may participate in it diplomatically, perhaps now and then suggesting things the young people might like to do together. She should be careful not to be an "arranger." Quietly and unobtrusively she keeps her weather eye open. Her daughter, or even her daughter and her "steady," may indicate a desire to talk it over with her. If so, the mother should welcome the chance. Then she will be deeply interested, even a bit enthusiastic, but seizing the opportunities to insert gentle and friendly cautions. She will know how to emphasize their youth, the penalties that have to be paid for foregoing education, the financial problems, the responsibilities of marriage, etc. Not too heavy an accent on "You will both forget all about this in a few months." Rather, a bit on the side of "Who can tell? Maybe later on you will both still be in love with each other. Then you can go ahead and you will be all the happier for having waited until the right time."

We know of quite a few teen-age love affairs which later on in life culminated in successful and happy marriages.

And so the pattern of girlhood romance, often indescribably beautiful, is woven with an infinite number of variations in design. Some of it is kept locked in the secret compartments of the psyche, but much of it spills over by behavior and often revealing words into the family circle, particularly if it is a happy home.

We have given only a few psychological potentials. There are many others. Children do not just grow up. Their emotional growth, even more than their flesh and blood growth, is deeply rooted in the home environmental soil. From this soil the human emotional plant draws its sustenance and the direction and nature of its growth is determined early and frequently cannot be changed. The psychological potentials must be nurtured and tended, unobtrusively, but carefully.

We have traced for mothers, parents and adults in general a childhood pattern. Imperfect as it is, it may be helpful. But let no parent be stuffy and superior about it, or disappointed or angry if it is not followed. Often children seem to flout it openly. The rebellion is part of their growing up, working out their own plan of life. Nevertheless, if the home situation is right and good, demonstrated more by behavior than by empty words, some of the lessons will be deeply graven on their plastic personalities and be utilized later for a richer and happier adult living.

We hope we have earned the right to ask all parents who have daughters to help them grow up into true, womanly women. They will be giving a rich and much-needed legacy to a troubled and confused world.

We have written this book not only with our minds, but also with our hearts. Among the many problems we have been and are asked to solve, none are more appealing and more important than the problems of daughters—babies, children, young women. Fairly often we have been successful in helping solve the problems. But we realize that what we and other psychiatrists have been able to do, after all, is a pitifully small contribution in the face of a great and urgent need. We feel that what we and others have learned should be widely disseminated and put at the disposal of mothers and fathers of daughters and, in fact, made available to everyone who is interested in their welfare. That is why we wrote this book.

The issue is of the utmost importance. We think it is critical. In the struggle between a free and an enslaved world, between democracy and dictatorship, each good mother and the mature daughters she produces are worth a company of soldiers. If there are enough good mothers, democracy will triumph.

Several years ago, the White House Conference on Children defined the "Rights of Children" as follows:

"From your earliest infancy we give you our love, so that you may grow with trust in yourself and others.

"We will recognize your worth as a person and we will help you to strengthen your sense of belonging.

"We will respect your right to be yourself and at the same time help you to understand the rights of others, so that you may experience cooperative living.

"We will help you develop initiative and imagination, so that you may have the opportunity freely to create.

"We will encourage your curiosity and your pride in workmanship, so that you may have the satisfaction that comes from achievement.

"We will provide the conditions for wholesome play that will add to your learning, to your social experience, and to your happiness.

"We will illustrate by precept and example the value of integrity and the importance of moral courage.

"We will encourage you always to seek the truth.

"We will open the way for you to enjoy the arts and to use them for deepening your understanding of life.

"We will work to rid ourselves of prejudice and discrimination, so that together we may achieve a truly democratic society.

"We will work to lift the standard of living and to improve our economic practices, so that you may have the material basis for a full life.

"We will provide you with rewarding educational opportunities, so that you may develop your talents and contribute to a better world.

"We will protect you against exploitation and undue hazards and help you grow in health and strength.

"We will work to conserve and improve family life and, as needed, to provide foster care according to your inherent rights.

"We will intensify our search for new knowledge in order to guide you more effectively as you develop your potentialities.

"As you grow from child to youth to adult, establishing a family life of your own and accepting larger social responsibilities, we will work with you to improve conditions for all children and youth."

These are the "Rights of Children." They are some of the things children are entitled to from adults. It is sad to reflect that comparatively few children receive these rights. Millions of children, particularly in underprivileged, deprived and dictatorial countries, do not get any of them.

These rights apply as much to girls as they do to boys. Perhaps more so. Certainly the need is greater. Girls will become the mothers of men and women. They cannot give more than they have, more than we give them.

Let us all, each one of us, mothers, fathers, every adult, do all we can to give girls their rights. For them and for their children, this gift will be more precious than money, stocks and bonds, mortgages and chattels. And it will outlast them.

Answers to Questionnaire

1.	Yes	24.	Yes	47.	No	70.	No
2.	No	25.	No	48.	No	71.	No
3.	No	26.	No	49.	No	72.	No
4.	No	27.	No	50.	No	73.	No
5.	No	28.	No	51.	No	74.	No
6.	Yes	29.	No	52.	No	75.	No
7.	No	30.	No	53.	No	76.	No
8.	Yes	31.	No	54.	No	77.	No
9.	Yes	32.	No	55.	No	78.	No
10.	No	33.	No	56.	No	79.	Yes
11.	No	34.	No	57.	Yes	80.	No
12.	No	35.	No	58.	Yes	81.	No
13.	Yes	36.	No	59.	Yes	82.	Yes
14.	No	37.	No	60.	Yes	83.	No
15.	No	38.	No	61.	No	84.	No
16.	No	39.	No	62.	No	85.	No
17.	No	40.	No	63.	No	86.	Yes
18.	No	41.	No	64.	No	87.	No
19.	No	42.	No	65.	No	88.	Yes
20.	Yes	43.	Yes	66.	No	89.	No
21.	No	44.	No	67.	No	90.	No
22.	No	45.	No	68.	No		
23.	No	46.	No	69.	No		